~Introducing Fiqh Series~
Vol.1

Introducing the *Fiqh* of Purification

باب الطهارة

من كتاب : الأدلة و البيان

على فقه أبي حنيفة النعمان

Written and compiled by
SAFARUK Z. CHOWDHURY

AD-DUHA
LONDON 2008

First edition 2008
Second Edition 2009
Updated Edition 2010

An educational publication from Ad-Duha London
Third Floor, 42 Fieldgate Street
London E1 1ES
E: info@duha.org.uk
W: www.duha.org.uk
T: 07891 421 925

Section	**Pages**

SECTION ONE: *ANJAS* (الأنجاس/Impurities):

§1. Preliminaries.
§2. Virtues of Cleanliness.
§3. Some terms.
§4. Water and its Types.
§5. Water and Various Injunctions.
§6. Impurities and its Types.
§7. Shari`a modes of Cleaning.
§8. *Istinja'* (الإستنجاء) – washing the private parts.
§9. Miscellaneous Injunctions.

SECTION TWO: *WUDU'* (الوضوء/Ablution):

§1. Preliminaries of *wudu'*.
§2. The definition of *wudu'*.
§3. The virtues of *wudu'*.
§4. Some outlines regarding *wudu'*.
§5. That which makes *wudu'* valid.
§6. The obligatory aspects of *wudu'*.
§7. The *sunna* aspects of *wudu'*.
§8. The *adab* (etiquettes) aspects of *wudu'*.
§9. That which is disliked in *wudu'*.
§10. That which invalidates the *wudu'*.
§11. That which does not invalidate the *wudu'*.
§12. Miscellaneous injunctions of *wudu'*.

SECTION THREE: *GHUSL* (الغسل/Ritual Bath):

§1. Preliminaries and definition of *Ghusl*.
§2. That which obligates the *Ghusl*.

MUQADDIMA
('INTRODUCTION')

الحمد لله حمداً يبلغ رضاه وصلى الله على أشرف من اجتباه
وعلى من صاحبه ووالاه وسلم تسليماً لا يدرك منتهاه.

———— ◆ ————

Praise be to Allah Most High; The Giver of this perfect and final Law for all times and abundant blessings upon our beloved Prophet, the Divine Mercy sent for humankind who embodied this perfect Law and implemented it for all to follow and who is the Light of guidance that has radiated the firmaments. Blessings too upon his noble companions who followed His blessed example in implementing this sacred law, his pure family and all those who follow them in creed and deed until the Final Day. **To proceed**:

- In our creedal postulations, we have the following articles:

71. "The Shari`a of Muhammad is the most perfect Shari`a and his religion has abrogated all other religions".[1]

[71] شريعته أكمل الشرائع و دينه ناسخ الأديان...

87. "No Muslim ever reaches

[87] و لا يصل العبد الى حيث يسقط

---

[1] See Shah `Abd al-Haqq al-Dihlawi, *Takmil al-Iman*, p.101.

a point where the commands and prohibitions no longer apply to him."[2]

عنه الأمر والنهي

- Our Sacred Law is perfect and it is from Allah.

- The revelation of our Sacred Law is for it to be implemented in all aspects of life and no-one is excused from following it.

- There are currents today that are challenging this classical understanding of the total implementation of our Sacred Law. This challenge has taken many different forms and guises such whether political actions in directly thwarting any localised movements to secure political authority for Islam and its systems or through indirect means such as sponsoring intellectual and academic dissent to problematize normative aspects of Islam.

- Muslims cannot severe their ties from the Law revealed by Allah and implemented practically by His beloved (Allah be pleased with him) because to do so would be to substitute Divine guidance with the predilection and caprice of man.

- It is thus incumbent upon all Muslims to learn the integrals related to their actions in all domains of their life and proceed on this basis. This is the study of 'fiqh' (فقه / 'Islamic positive law' / 'knowledge of Islamic law').

- The gálactico of scholars from al-Azhar, the supreme master in *hadith* scholarship al-Hafiz Imam Ibn Hajar

---

[2] See Shah `Abd al-Haqq al-Dihlawi, *Takmil al-Iman*, p.147.

al-`Asqalani (d.852/1449)[3] comments on the noble *hadith* of the humanity's mercy our blessed Prophet (abundant peace and blessings be upon him): **"Whoever Allah wishes good for, He endows them with knowledge of *fiqh* of the Religion"** stating:[4]

[...] وفي ذلك بيان ظاهر لفضل العلماء على سائر الناس، ولفضل التفقه في الدين على

سائر العلوم...

"...and in this [narration] is a clear exposition of the superiority of the scholars over the rest of the people and the superiority of *fiqh* over all other sciences."[5]

- *Fiqh*[6] ('knowledge of Islamic legal rulings' / 'Islamic positive law') is considered to be the paramount discipline in Islam, the 'queen of the sciences'.

- There are many statements of the *Sahaba* (companions of the Prophet) and early righteous scholars (*al-salaf*) that uphold this for example:

[1] Anas Ibn Malik (ra):

أنا أبو عبد الله محمد بن عبد الواحد بن أحمد الطرفي المعدل بالكرخ، نا عمر بن إبراهيم

بن مردويه الكرخي، نا ابن جعفر النجيرمي، نا أحمد بن سعيد الثقفي، نا أبو روح الهيثم بن

---

[3] For more on him, see A. A. Rahmani, *The Life and Works of Ibn Hajar al-Asqalani*, Islamic Foundation Bangladesh, 2000.

[4] Bukhari, *Sahih* (#3116).

[5] Ibn Hajar al-`Asqalani, *Fath al-Bari Sharh Sahih al-Bukhari*, 1:164-164.

[6] For a discussion of the term 'fiqh', refer to A. Hasan, *The Early Development of Islamic Jurisprudence*, pp.1-11 and I. A. K. Nyazee, *Islamic Jurisprudence*, pp.18-24.

برزخ ، نا إبراهيم بن ميسرة عن أنس بن مالك رضي الله عنه، قال : قال رسول الله : إن لكل

أمة رهبانية، وإن رهبانية أمتي الجماعات والجمعات وتعليم بعضهم بعضاً شرائع الدين...

"From Anas b. Malik[7] (God be pleased with him) who said: 'every nation has religious leaders and the religious leaders of my community are a group of people who teach each other the obligatory acts (*shara'i '*) of the Religion'."[8]

أنا عبد الغفار بن محمد المؤدب، أنا عمر بن أحمد الواعظ، نا عبد الله بن عمر بن سعيد

الطالقاني، نا عمار بن عبد الحميد، نا محمد بن مقاتل الرازي عن أبي العباس جعفر بن

هارون عن سمعان بن المهدي عن أنس رضي الله عنه ، قال : قال رسول الله : أفضل العلم

الذي يحتاج إليه الناس.

قلت : وأعظم ما بالناس الحاجة إليه من العلوم الفقه فلا علم أفضل منه .

"From Anas b. Malik (God be pleased with him) who said: The Messenger of God (God bless him and give him peace) said: **'the best knowledge is that which the people need.'**

I say [s: meaning the author al-Khatib al-Baghdadi]: the greatest science or knowledge the people need is *fiqh* as no science is better or more excellent than it."[9]

---

[7] One of the last surviving companions whose life almost bridged the entire seventh century. A profuse transmitter of *hadith* from the Prophet and a highly revered individual. He died in Basra aged over one hundred years. See G. H. A. Juynboll, s.v. *Encyclopedia of Canonical Hadith*, pp.131-133.

[8] al-Khatib al-Baghdadi, *al-Faqih wa 'l-Mutafaqqih*, 1:144-145.

[9] al-Khatib al-Baghdadi, *al-Faqih wa 'l-Mutafaqqih*, 1:145.

فقد روى يحيى بن سليمان عن ابن وهب، قال : سمعت مالكاً يقول : كثير من هذه
الأحاديث ضلالة لقد خرجت مني أحاديث لوددت إني ضربت بكل حديث منها سوطين
وإني لم أحدث به .

"Yahya b. Sulayman narrated from Ibn Wahb who said: I
heard Malik [b. Anas][10] say: 'Many of these *hadiths* are [a
cause for] misguidance;[11] some *hadiths* were narrated by me
and I wish that for each of them I had been flogged with a
stick twice. I certainly no longer narrate them!'"[12]

حدثنا عبد الرحمن حدثني ابي نا هارون بن سعيد الايلي بمصر قال سمعت ابن وهب –
وذكر اختلاف الاحاديث والروايات فقال: لولا اني لقيت مالكا والليث لضللت.

"…Ibn Wahb said regarding the differences over *hadiths* and
their transmissions that: 'were I not to have met Malik or al-
Layth [b. Sa`d], I would surely have been misguided…'"[13]

[2] Ibn al-Mubarak:

وقال أبو وهب ومحمد بن مزاحم سمعت بن المبارك يقول أفقه الناس أبو حنيفة ما رأيت في
الفقه مثله و قال أيضا لولا أن الله تعالى أغاثني بأبي حنيفة وسفيان كنت كسائر الناس...

"Abu Wahb and Muhammad b. Mazahim said: I heard Ibn
al-Mubarak[14] say: 'The most knowledgeable jurist is Abu

---

[10] One of the early traditionists and jurist of Medina whose compilation
entitled *Muwatta'* is the earliest surviving collection of legal traditions.
He developed his own legal methodology comprising one of the four
orthodox legal Schools. J. Schacht, "Malik b. Anas", *EI*[1], 5:205-209.

[11] Meaning they can mislead and cause misunderstanding unless correctly
understood.

[12] al-Khatib al-Baghdadi, *al-Faqih wa 'l-Mutafaqqih*, 2:158.

[13] See Ibn Abi Hatim, *al-Jarh wa 'l-Ta`dil*, 1:23; al-Qadi `Iyad, *Tartib al-
Madarik*, 2:427; Ibn Hibban, *Kitab al-Majruhin*, 1:42 (introduction); Ibn
Abi Zayd, *al-Jami` fi 'l-Sunan*, pp.118-119 and Ibn `Abd al-Barr, *al-
Intiqa'*, p.61.

Hanifa. I have not seen the likes of him.' [Ibn al-Mubarak] also said: 'If God (Most High) had not rescued me with Abu Hanifa and Sufyan [al-Thawri][15] I would have been like the rest of the common people'."[16]

[3] Yahya Ibn Ma`in:

وقال أحمد بن علي بن سعيد القاضي سمعت يحيى بن معين يقول سمعت يحيى بن سعيد القطان يقول لا تكذب الله ما سمعنا أحسن من رأى أبي حنيفة وقد أخذنا بأكثر اقواله...

"Ahmad b. `Ali b. Sa`id al-Qadi said: I heard Yahya b. Ma`in say: I heard Sa`id al-Qattani say: 'We do not belie God. We never heard better than the legal opinions of Abu Hanifa and we followed most of his positions'."[17]

- Through *fiqh* therefore, one attains correct knowledge of actions required by the Creator from His servants so that He (SWT) can be validly and properly worshipped.

---

[14] A famous ascetic and *mujahid*. He was also a traditionist of Persian origin as well as a profuse memorizer and collector of *hadith* but saw the pitfalls in attempting to understand them without the requisite legal knowledge. He is said to have compiled approximately 120,000 *hadiths*. Cf. al-Subki's al-*Tabaqat al-Shafi`iyyat al-Kubra*, 2:128. See also al-Tabari (trans. E. Landau-Tasseron), *Biographies of the Prophet's Companions and their Successors*, pp.263-264, fn.1170.

[15] Theologian, jurist and famous ascetic of the second century who enjoys immense authority in Islamic pietistic literature as well as traditionist discourse. His reliability is unanimously agreed upon by Muslim scholars as well as his prodigious memory and accuracy. M. Plessner, "Sufyan al-Thawri", *EI*[1], 7:500-502.

[16] Ibn Hajar al-`Asqalani, *Tahdhib al-Tahdhib*, 10:450.

[17] Ibn Hajar al-`Asqalani, *Tahdhib al-Tahdhib*, 10:450 and al-Dhahabi, *Tadhkirat al-Huffaz*, 1:307.

- In Islam, every individual is duty-bound to learn the integrals related to h/her actions and will be in commission of a sin in failing to do so.

- This book is a small contribution for servicing this duty. It is a summary of the key injunctions, terms and concepts related to the Chapter of Purification (*kitab al-tahara*) according the legal school (*madhhab*) of the noble jurist, *mujtahid mutlaq* Nu`man Ibn Thabit al-Imam al-A`zam Abu Hanifa (Allah be pleased with him).[18] He is in this author's humble opinion, the greatest jurist that has ever lived.

- The book has been written primarily for intermediary class format hence its brevity as well as citations of long passages from the manuals of *fiqh*. Some topics have been omitted (e.g. injunctions pertaining to wells and women's issues) and complex juristic discussion-points avoided.

- This book can, however, be read and studied with reliable scholars or persons familiar with this chapter of Islamic injunctions and each section is self-contained and referenced for further reading and discussion.

- This is not a book that seeks to present the legal evidences adduced by the jurists of the Hanafi school and neither are there mention of the modes of deduction and derivation from the Hanafi legal methodology (*usul*); it is merely a collection of injunctions pertaining to integrals that each person must know so as to build a foundation for further pursuance and study.

---

[18] See Ibn Khallikan's *Biographical Dictionary*, 3:555-574 for an account of his life.

***We ask Allah *ta`la* for His Help in fulfilling our
obligations***
Amin!

SECTION 1: *ANJAS* ('IMPURITIES')

———— ♦ ————

§1. Preliminaries

- Allah (SWT) states in the Qur'an:

...وثيابك فطهر 🕋

{...*and purify your garments*}[19]

- Sayyiduna Salman al-Farisi (Allah be well pleased with him) was reportedly asked by an anonymous interlocutor:

"Salman was asked: 'Your Prophet (Allah bless him and give him peace) has taught you everything, even how to defecate?' Salman replied: 'Indeed. He has prohibited us from facing the *qibla* when defecating or urinating or to cleanse ourselves with the right hand, to cleanse ourselves with less than three stones or to cleanse ourselves with a piece of dung or bone'."[20]

قيل لسلمان : قد علمكم نبيكم صلى الله

عليه وسلم كل شيء، حتى الخراءة ؟ فقال

سلمان : أجل، نهانا أن نستقبل القبلة

بغائط أو بول، أو أن نستنجي باليمين، أو

أن يستنجي أحدنا بأقل من ثلاثة أحجار،

أو نستنجي برجيع أو بعظم.

- Islam is a faith emphatic on purity.[21]

---

[19] Qur'an 74:4.
[20] Tirmidhi, *Sunan* (#16).
[21] M. H. Katz, *Body of Text: The Emergence of the Sunni Law of Ritual Purity*, p.1.

- Islamic ritual law is elaborate and highly intricate and the noble *fuqaha'* who have delineated the rules and injunctions (*ahkam*) pertaining to that area of law have discussed this at extreme length.[22]

- Indeed, the legal discussions, evidences and derivations are bewildering to any who is not familiar with the objective, nature and functioning of Islamic Law (*al-shari`a*).[23]

- Islamic Law encompasses law, rituals, devotion, doctrine, ethics, politics, economics and spirituality and hence is comprehensive than how law is understood in the west.[24]

- Islamic injunctions extend to all areas involving human actions from as specific as cleaning one's private parts to as broad as running a state.

- No other major world tradition requires its adherents to be intimately acquainted with matters of hygiene and cleanliness than Islam.[25]

- Spirituality is intimately woven into the mundane and sensual giving rise to the elaborate domain of body hygienical jurisprudence.

- Ze'ev Maghen remarks:

  > ...I will argue that the laws of *tahara* in general... have rather helped to preserve an

---

[22] Ibid, pp.1-2.

[23] Ibid, p.1.

[24] For outlines of Islamic Law and how it operates, see W. B. Hallaq, *An Introduction to Islamic Law*, pp.5-71.

[25] See Z. Maghen, *Virtues of the Flesh: Passion and Purity in Early Islamic Jurisprudence*, pp.ix-2 and 12-13.

affinity between the material and the spiritual in the Islamic ethos and this in a number of different ways. First, the vast and intricate network of purity-for-prayer laws has bound anatomy to theology forever in the consciousness of the Muslim intellectual elite. The greatest minds of every Islamic age, from followers to *fuqaha'*, from *murabitun* to *mutakallimun*, have had no choice but to do what Socrates inveighed so heavily against: 'to associate with the body, and care for it and love it, to be beguiled by the body and its passions and pleasures'. They must needs delve into and discuss unabashedly the kisses and caresses and foreplay and coition, the manifold secretions and excretions and fluids which form the visceral and unmediated physicality of man.[26]

• Marion Katz explains this phenomenon as follows:

It is a truism that Islamic Law (the Shari`a) is a comprehensive system encompassing all aspects of life. Not limiting itself to public or enforceable norms, it provides guidance for the most intimate and most apparently trivial details of the believer's private conduct. The Shari`a's unflinching attention to the least sublime aspects of human experience has often, as the above anecdote suggests, been met with the incomprehension of outside observers. Its exhaustive examination of the minutiae of the believer's biological functions, up to and including the details of elimination and sexual behaviour has provoked the mirth of seventh-century Arabians and twentieth-century Americans alike. The classical

---

[26] Maghen, *Virtues of the Flesh*, p.20.

Islamic sources themselves, however, consistently insist that false modesty should not prevent thorough inquiry into this area of law. "God is not ashamed of the truth [Qur'an 33:53]", an Ansari woman declares to the Prophet in an early report; "how should I wash myself after menstruation?" "How praiseworthy are the women of the Ansar", the Prophet's wife `A'isha is supposed to have said, remembering this event: "shame did not prevent them from informing themselves about their religion...[27]

- Thus, Islamic injunctions and laws are effective in all areas of human action.

- There is no problem or reality that Islam fails to address and so Muslims must seek the Islamic ruling on any matter in which they seek to undertake an action.

- In what follows below will be an outline of the basic concepts and injunctions related to purities/impurities (*anjas*) within the school of Imam al-A`zam Abu Hanifa (Allah be pleased with him).

- The primary text used as a basis for this section is the primer on Hanafi devotional injunctions entitled *Nur al-Idah* ('The Light of Clarification') by the regional Qadi of Egypt Imam al-Shurunbulali with his own interlinear commentary of the manual entitled *Maraqi al-Falah* ('The Ascent to Felicity').

---

[27] Katz, *Body of Text*, p.1.

§2. The Virtues of Cleanliness

- Islam insists on religious purity and cleanliness and the Islamic faith is distinct and unique in its formalisation of specific rituals.

- There are innumerable Qur'anic verses and narrations (*ahadith*) that expound the virtues of cleanliness and classical commentators have explained them in great detail.

- Below are four examples:

[1] Allah loves those who purify themselves:

إِنَّ ٱللَّهَ يُحِبُّ ٱلتَّوَّابِينَ وَيُحِبُّ لَا تَقُمْ فِيهِ أَبَداً لَّمَسْجِدٌ أُسِّسَ عَلَى ٱلْمُتَطَهِّرِينَ ۝ ٱلتَّقْوَىٰ مِنْ أَوَّلِ يَوْمٍ أَحَقُّ أَن تَقُومَ فِيهِ رِجَالٌ يُحِبُّونَ أَن يَتَطَهَّرُواْ وَٱللَّهُ يُحِبُّ ٱلْمُطَّهِّرِينَ ۝

{...in it are men who love to clean and purify themselves. And Allah loves those who keep themselves clean and pure}.[28]

{Indeed, Allah loves those who turn to him in repentance and those who keep themselves clean and pure}.[29]

[2] Allah ascribed purity to himself:

"Indeed, Allah is pure and He loves purity, He is clean and loves cleanliness, Most graceful and kind and loves kindness and Most Generous

إن الله طيب يحب الطيب نظيف يحب النظافة كريم يحب الكرم جواد يحب

---

[28] Qur'an 9:108.
[29] Qur'an 2:222.

and loves generosity…"[30]   الجود...

[3] Paradise is conditional upon purity:

"Islam is purity and cleanliness so clean yourselves. None but the pure and clean will enter Paradise…"[31]

الإسلام نظيف فتنظفوا فإنه لا يدخل الجنة إلا نظيف

[4] Cleanliness is linked to true belief:

"Purity is part of faith…"[32]   الطهور شطر الإيمان...

- Cleanliness and ritual purity therefore are essential states of a Muslim; something h/she has to perpetually maintain.

- Purity is thus substantively integrated into the Muslim faith and practice.

Note:

- **Islamic legal maxims (*qawa`id fiqhiyya*):** there are a number of assumed maxims or rules pertaining to discussions on water and purity that need to be mentioned and they include:

  1. Water is assumed to be clean and pure until and unless one has strong doubts it is filthy or impure.[33]

---

[30] See Tirmidhi, *Sunan* (#2799).
[31] See al-Haythami, *Majma` al-Zawa'id*, 5:135.
[32] See Muslim, *Sahih* (#328).
[33] Based on the principle:

2. Certainty is not eroded by doubt or suspicion and so the assumed purity of water will remain until one is sure it is otherwise.[34]

3. A strong doubt or suspicion is equal to certainty.[35]

• Correct application of these principles enables new situations to be resolved as well as personal doubts to be dispelled.

الأصل الطهارة في كل شئ

al-asl al-tahara fi kulli shay' ('the assumed norm is that all things are considered pure').

[34] Based on the principles:

الأصل الإباحة إلا ما دل الدليل على نجاسته أو تحريمه...

[1] *al-asl al-ibaha illa ma dalla al-dalil `ala najasatihi aw tahrimihi* ('the assumed norm is permissibility of using anything, except when there exists an evidence indicative of its impurity or prohibition') and

اليقين لا يزال بالشك

[2] *al-yaqin la yuzalu bi'l-shakk* ('certainty is not eroded by doubt').
[35] Based on the principle:

والظن الغالب ينزل منزلة اليقين

§3. Some Terms

- The reason for the use of the word 'kitab' (كِتَاب/ 'domain', 'book', 'chapter') in manuals of Islamic sacred Law is in order to suggest the comprehensiveness and encompassing and broad character of the discussions because they comprise of a collection of legal injunctions and legal particulars and cases.[36]

- The word 'tahara' / الطَّهَارَةُ linguistically means 'cleansing' (al-nazafa / النَّظَافَةُ) and its opposite is 'filth' (al-dans / الدَّنَسُ). In the specified terminology of the jurists, it means washing certain limbs (a`da' makhsusa / أَعْضَاءٍ مَخْصُوصَةٍ) and its opposite is ritual impurity (hadath / الْحَدَثُ).[37]

- There are at least three key terms worthy of note pertaining to ritual purification:[38]

[1] **The purifier** (mutahhir/مُطَهِّر): the purifying agent, e.g. water or in its absence, dry earth (sa`id).

---

[36] See Shaykh Zadah, *Majma` al-Anhur*, 1:1-2:

الْكِتَابُ فِي اللُّغَةِ هُوَ الْجَمْعُ يُقَالُ كَتَبْت الشَّيْءَ أَيْ جَمَعْته وَمِنْهُ الْكِتَابَةُ وَهِيَ جَمْعُ الْحُرُوفِ بَعْضِهَا إِلَى بَعْضٍ، فَقَوْلُهُ كِتَابُ الطَّهَارَةِ أَيْ جَمْعُ مَسَائِلِ الطَّهَارَةِ وَفِي الشَّرْعِ عِبَارَةٌ عَنْ الشَّمْلِ وَالْإِحَاطَةِ وَهُمَا لَفْظَانِ مُتَرَادِفَانِ بِمَعْنًى وَاحِدٍ، وَقِيلَ هُمَا مُتَغَايِرَانِ وَهُوَ الصَّحِيحُ [...] وَالطَّهَارَةُ فِي اللُّغَةِ هِيَ النَّظَافَةُ وَعَكْسُهَا الدَّنَسُ وَفِي الشَّرْعِ عِبَارَةٌ عَنْ غَسْلِ أَعْضَاءٍ مَخْصُوصَةٍ وَعَكْسُهَا الْحَدَثُ وَيُقَالُ أَيْضًا عِبَارَةٌ عَنْ رَفْعِ حَدَثٍ أَوْ إِزَالَةِ نَجَسٍ حَتَّى يُسَمَّى الدِّبَاغُ وَالتَّيَمُّمُ طَهَارَةً وَأَعَمُّ مِنْ هَذَا أَنْ يُقَالَ عِبَارَةٌ عَنْ إِيصَالِ مُطَهِّرٍ إِلَى مَحَلٍّ يَجِبُ تَطْهِيرُهُ أَوْ يُنْدَبُ إِلَيْهِ وَالْمُطَهِّرُ هُوَ الْمَاءُ عِنْدَ وُجُودِهِ وَالصَّعِيدُ عِنْدَ عَدَمِهِ، وَالطَّهَارَةُ عَلَى ضَرْبَيْنِ حَقِيقِيَّةٌ وَهِيَ الطَّهَارَةُ بِالْمَاءِ وَحُكْمِيَّةٌ وَهِيَ التَّيَمُّمُ، وَالطَّهَارَةُ بِالْمَاءِ عَلَى ضَرْبَيْنِ خَفِيفَةٌ كَالْوُضُوءِ وَغَلِيظَةٌ كَالْغُسْلِ مِنْ الْجَنَابَةِ وَالْحَيْضِ وَالنِّفَاسِ.

[37] Shaykh Zadah, *Majma` al-Anhur*, 1:2.
[38] Shaykh Zadah, *Majma` al-Anhur*, 1:2.

[2] **Purification act** (*tathir*/تَطْهِير): Pouring water on specific limbs or the entire body. This is of two types:[39]

[a] *Hukmiyya* / حُكْمِيَّة / *legal*: e.g. washing or 'cleansing' through *tayammum* ('dry ablution').

[b] *Haqiqiyya* / حَقِيقِيَّة / *actual*: e.g. washing or cleansing with actual water;[40]

[3] **A state of ritual Impurity** (*hadath*/حَدَث): e.g. a state requiring either *wudu'* (= *hadath asghar* ['minor ritual impurity']) or *ghusl* (= *hadath akbar* ['major ritual impurity']). This is of two types:

[a] *khafifa* (خَفِيفَة /'light cleansing', e.g. *wudu'*)

[b] *Ghaliza* (غَلِيظَة /'heavy cleansing', e.g. full bath).

---

[39] Shaykh Zadah, *Majma' al-Anhur*, 1:2.
[40] Shaykh Zadah, *Majma' al-Anhur*, 1:2.

§4. Water and its Types

———— ◆ ————

- al-Shurunbulali in *Nur al-Idah* outlines the basic categories of water (*al-ma'*):

"There are five categories of water: [1] The first is that water which is pure and can purify something else and is nothing disliked in using it... [2] The second is that water which is pure and can purify something else although it is disliked to use it... [3] The third is water that is pure but cannot be used to purify something else... [4] The fourth is water that is considered impure... and [5] The fifth is water that is doubtful in terms of its purity..."[41]

ثم المياه على خمسة أقسام الأول طاهر مطهر غير مكروه [...] والثاني طاهر مطهر مكروه [...] والثالث طاهر غير مطهر [...] والرابع ماء نجس [...] والخامس ماء مشكوك في طهوريته...

- Thus from the above we have 5 types of water each with their relevant scope and applications:

Sources of water include:

1. Rain,
2. oceans,
3. rivers,
4. streams,
5. lakes,
6. wells,

---

[41] al-Shurunbulali, *Nur al-Idah*, pp.23-26.

7. snow,
8. hail and
9. springs, etc.

- Water from these sources is considered absolutely pure (*tahir*) and make up category [1] below.[42]

Types of Water

[1]	[2]	[3]	[4]	[5]
Pure and purifying[43]	**Pure and purifying but disliked to use**[44]	**Pure but not purifying**	**Impure water**	**Pure, but doubtful in whether it purifies**
e.g. commonly used water from taps, bottles, pumps, etc. It can be used for ritual cleansing i.e. for *wudu'* and	e.g. if a cat drinks from it (if the water is a small quantity).	e.g. water used for the performance of *wudu'* and *ghusl* (bath), i.e. ritual cleansing.	e.g. when an impurity has fallen in it (when the water is still).	e.g. water which a donkey, pony or mule has drank from.[45]

---

[42] al-Shurunbulali, *Nur al-Idah*, p.23.

[43] By the term 'purifying' (*mutahhir*), it means any type of water permitted by the Shari`a to clean other objects with.

[44] Here, the level of dislike (*karaha*) is not emphatic (*tahrimi*) but non-emphatic (*tanzihi*) in that if absolute pure water is available, it should be used. See Wahba, *Sabil al-Falah Sharh Nur al-Idah*, p.13f.

[45] The reason for the ruling of doubt extended to cases involving mules, ponies and donkeys in general is due to the conflicting textual evidences related to whether their meat is lawful to consume. See M. Wahba, *Sabil al-Falah Sharh Nur al-Idah*, p.17.

ghusl
(bath) and
actual
cleansing,
i.e.
removing
dirt, filth,
impurity.

- Water is also classified according to other various types:

Other Types of Water

[A]	**[B]**	**[C]**	**[D]**
Used water (*al-musta`mal*)[46]	**Left-over water (*al-su'r*)**	**Sweat**	**Entrapped Water**
e.g. water that falls off the body when doing *wudu'* or *ghusl*. This cannot be used for religious mandatory cleansing (*najasa hukmiyya*) but can	e.g. water that remains after a human (Christian, Jew, *mushrik*, etc.) or an animal has drank from it.	Sweat takes the ruling (*hukm*) of saliva[48] and left-over water. Any animal whose saliva	e.g. rosewater, coconut water, tree water, juices in the fruit, vinegar and gasoline, etc.

---

[46] 'Used water' is defined as:

"Water is considered to be 'used' right after it separates from the body..." See al-Shurunbulali, *Nur al-Idah*, p.24 and Ibn `Abidin, *Radd al-Muhtar*, 1:38. See Imam Ahmad Reza Khan, *al-Tirs al-Mu`addal fi Hadd al-Ma' al-Musta`mal*, pp.35-112 for a detailed discussion of this.

ويصير الماء مستعملا بمجرد انفصاله عن
الجسد...

be used to clean actual/substantive filth ([*najasa haqiqiyya*] e.g. urine, excrements, blood, etc).[47]	Any kind of animal permitted to eat, if it drinks from a little pure water, the left-over water is considered pure. Any kind of animal not permitted to eat, if it drinks from a little amount of pure water, the left-over water is considered impure. Any kind of domesticated animal or wild & domesticated bird if it drinks from a little pure water, the left-over water is considered	and left-over water is considered impure, subsequently its sweat will be considered impure. Any animal whose saliva and left-over water is considered pure, subsequently its sweat will be considered pure.

---

[48] al-Shurunbulali, *Maraqi al-Sa`adat*, p.65.

[47] See W. Zuhayli, *al-Fiqh al-Islami wa Adillatuhu*, 1:149-150 for a discussion on the differences between these two types of impurities. Cf. also Katz, *Body and Text*, pp.147-149 and Maghen, *Virtues of the Flesh*, pp.7-8, n.13.

disliked.

Water left-
over from a
donkey or
mule is
considered
doubtful but
can be used
for *wudu'*.

§5. Water and Various Injunctions

- A small amount of water is considered to be a total of 10 by 10 arm's length (total circumference being 63 arms length) and where if one were to scoop water up the bottom would be seen. Any *najasa* ('filth') that falls into this amount will automatically make the water impure even if one does not see any affects in colour, taste or smell.[49]

- A large amount of water is considered to be that amount where if one stirs water on one side of the water, the other is not affected by the ripples or that which is more than 10 by 10 arm's length (total circumference being more than 63 arms length).[50]

- If water loses two out of three of its properties (which are colour, taste and smell) to another *liquid substance*, then it will be considered unfit for use as it would have become dominated.[51]

- If water loses its property of fluidity or thinness and looseness to another *solid substance*, then it will be considered unfit for use as it would have become dominated.

- If water has been cooked with other substances (lentils, meats, etc.), such that its essence has changed, it cannot be used.[52]

- If water is mixed with solids (e.g. fruits, stones, leaves, etc.) such that its property of fluidity or

---

[49] al-Shurunbulali, *Nur al-Idah*, pp.25-26.
[50] al-Shurunbulali, *Nur al-Idah*, p.25.
[51] al-Shurunbulali, *Nur al-Idah*, pp.24-25.
[52] al-Shurunbulali, *Nur al-Idah*, p.25.

thinness and looseness is not affected, the water may be used.[53]

- If water from canals, ponds, small areas, etc. has an impurity in it, then unless there is change in its properties of smell, taste and colour, the water will remain pure to use.[54]

- Flowing water (from streams, seas, rivers, etc.) is always pure.

---

[53] al-Shurunbulali, *Nur al-Idah*, pp.24-25.
[54] Sh. M. I. M. Madani, *The Book of Purification*, pp.70-74.

§6. Impurities and its Types

- There are two broad categories of filth (*najasa*) delineated by the *fuqaha'*:

[1] *Najasa haqiqiyya*: actual filth/impurity that is observable or knowable from the reality, e.g. excrement, faeces, urine, blood, etc. This is itself of two types:[55]

[1]	[2]
***Khafifa*/light**	***Ghaliza*/strong**
This refers to the urine of lawful (*halal*) animals and the droppings of forbidden (*haram*) birds.[56]	This refers to the urine and flowing blood of humans and unlawful animals, wine and droppings of chicken and ducks.[57]

[2] *Najasa hukmiyya*: a state of impurity that is considered so by the Shari`a even though it may not actually appear to be the case. This is also of two types:

[1]	[2]
hadath akbar **('major ritual impurity')**	***hadath asghar*** **('minor ritual impurity')**
This is when one requires a full purification bath (*ghusl*).	This is when one requires the ritual ablution (*wudu'*).[58]

---

[55] Ibid, pp.87-88.
[56] Ibid, p.89.
[57] Ibid, p.90.
[58] Ibid, pp.87-88.

- The means of washing any type of filth or impurity (*najas*) whether *khafifa* or *ghaliza* is to wash the object with water three times and in the case of clothes to wash it three times with a rinse (squeeze) at each wash.[59]

- Below is a table of some common impurities (*najasa*) and their ruling and method of cleaning:[60]

Substance (from humans)	Type of Impurity	Ruling	Method of Cleaning
Semen (includes *wadhi* & *madhi*)	*Ghaliza*/strong	Impure	If wet then wash away if dry then it can be scraped off.
Flowing blood	*Ghaliza*/strong	Impure	Washing it away with water until the filth is removed.
Swine/alcohol (all parts)	*Ghaliza*/strong	Impure	_____
Human urine	*Ghaliza*/strong	Impure	Washing it away if it is on clothes while rinsing it each time.
Human faeces	*Ghaliza*/strong	Impure	Washing it away if it is on clothes while rinsing

---

[59] Ibid, p.90.
[60] Ibid, pp.90-119.

it each time.

| Human vomit | *Ghaliza*/strong | Impure | Washing it away if it is on clothes while rinsing it each time |

- Other strong impurities include:

    1. Body parts of live animals.[61]
    2. Dead animals/carcasses (*mayta*).[62]
    3. Fats of dead animals.[63]
    4. Un-tanned hide of a dead animal.[64]
    5. Faeces and urine of animals unlawful to eat.
    6. Flowing blood of animals.[65]

- Light filth include:

    1. Urine of a horse.[66]
    2. Urine of non-predatory animals (e.g. cow, sheep).[67]
    3. Faecal matter of non-edible flying birds (e.g. hawk, falcon).[68]

- **Excusable filth**: in principle all amount or degree of filth has to be cleaned. However, there is a degree excusable for prayer only as mentioned by the Hanafi

---

[61] Abu Dawud, *Sunan* (#2475).
[62] Qur'an 2:173.
[63] Although some permit its use for soaps, etc.
[64] Abu Dawud, *Sunan* (#3599).
[65] Qur'an 6:145.
[66] al-Shurunbulali, *Nur al-Idah*, p.85.
[67] al-Shurunbulali, *Nur al-Idah*, p.85.
[68] al-Shurunbulali, *Nur al-Idah*, p.85.

fuqaha' and this is determined to be the size of a dirham coin (approximately 1.5 inches).

- The reasoning is as follows:

P1. `Aisha mentioned a *hadith* permitting the use of clay or stones to clean one's bottom after going to the toilet.[69]

P2. This means that filth can be wiped dry and not washed with water if it has not spread beyond the orifice (if it did, it has to be washed).[70]

P3. The approximate area of the orifice for excretion is appr. measured at 1.5inches (= dirham coin).

C1. *Therefore*, strong filth the size of a dirham (= appr. 1.5 inches) is excused and does not have to be washed.

- The name of a coin was thus used to specify the amount of excusable filth without mentioning the orifice:

"The scholars did not think it appropriate to mention the name of the excretory place, so they specified it with the size of a dirham instead."[71]   استقبحوا ذكر المقاعد في مجالسهم فكنوا عنها بالدرهم...

- Light filth less than a quarter of the full clothes is excused and this is determined by the minimum area

---

[69] Abu Dawud, *Sunan* (#63).
[70] Tirmidhi, *Sunan* (#19).
[71] Quoted in Madani, *The Book of Purification*, p.133.

required to be covered for prayer (which is the area from the navel to the knees).[72]

- However, the rule is **all** filth must be cleaned whether light/*khafif* or hard/*ghaliz*.

---

[72] al-Shurunbulali, *Nur al-Idah*, pp.85-86.

§7. Shari`a Modes of Cleaning Impurities

- Below is a table with basic modes of cleaning for different types of materials and surfaces:[73]

1	2	3	4
Grounds (floors, patios, steps, etc.)	**Non-absorbent Surfaces (glass, metals, plastics, etc.)** **& Solids (condiments)**	**Clothes (fabrics, cloths, light materials, etc.)**	**Heavy Materials/solids (carpets, rugs, heavy materials etc.)**
If loose dirt is on the ground, e.g. dry dirt, dry dust or general loose objects, scraping, sweeping, dusting, wiping or washing is sufficient.	Wiping the surface clean is sufficient otherwise washing the surface will be required.	Washing the impurity as many times as is necessary until the impurity is removed (although there is no problem if stains remain or a smell lingers).	Washed manually or with machines ensuring it is dried sufficiently between each wash such that the water does not drip from the material.
If it is wet impurities on the surface, e.g. urine, vomit, etc, if it dries up completely then it is considered pure if it is	Butter, yogurts, jams or general condiments are purified by simply removing the contaminated part and its surroundings. The rest will be considered pure.	Dried impurity requires three washes with a rinse (squeeze) between each wash.	

---

[73] Madani, *The Book of Purification*, pp.119-122.

not dry then
it has to be
washed.[74]

Some Basic Application
of *Fiqh* Principles – *Thick Materials*

Scenario A: *Impurity on thick materials*:

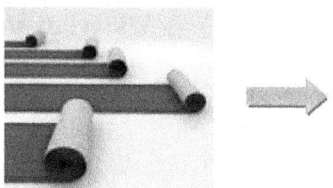

If any *impurity that cannot be seen after it dries up* (e.g. urine) falls on a thick material such as the carpets, rugs and heavy fabrics that cannot be squeezed then that would not be permitted for prayer on it/with it unless it is purified appropriately.

Method of cleaning: there are three methods to clean these tough and thick fabrics:

[1] Pour water over the area then dry the area with a cloth or sponge such that the material no-longer drips.

[2] Estimate how much water will be needed to wash the area by immersing the area in a utensil and filling it up until the impure area is covered. If it is a litre, say, then 3 litres of water will be needed to wash it and then dry it.

[3] If the impurity is such that it can be seen even after drying up, then one can simply pour water over the area until it is washed away or disappears. Whatever stain is left over is not given any consideration.

- al-Tahtawi, *Hashiyah*, p.159:

المرئية ما يرى بعد الجفاف وغير المرئية ما لا يرى بعدد، كذا في غاية البيان

"Visible means that which can be seen after the process of drying up and non-visible is when it cannot be seen after drying up [...]"

- In *al-Fatawa al-Hindiyyah*, 1:42 it states:

لو عصر بعدد لا يسيل منه الماء، ويعتبر في كل شخص قوته، وفي غير رواية الأصول :يكتفي بالعصر مرة، وهو أرفق، كذا في النكافي وفي النوازل وعليه الفتوى، كذا في التتارخانية والأول أحوط، هكذا في المحيط ... (وبعد أسطر) ... وما لا ينعصر يطهر بالغسل ثلاث مرات والتجفيف في كل مرة؛ لأن للتجفيف أثرا في استخراج النجاسة، وحد التجفيف أن يخليه حتى ينقطع التقاطر ولا يشترط به اليبس، هكذا في التبيين

"[...] whatever cannot be squeezed, that material is purified by washing it three times but with 'drying' (*tajfif*) in between every wash... and what is meant by 'drying' is is to leave it until it does not drip and <u>not that it has to be fully dried up</u> and this is what is mentioned in *al-Tabyin*."

---

[74] Ibn Abi Shayba, *al-Musannaf*, 1:40:

"From Abu Qilaba who said: 'When the earth dries up, it becomes clean'..."

عن أبي قلابة : اذا جفت الأرض فقد زكت...

Some Basic Application
of *Fiqh* Principles – *Earthen surface*

Scenario A: *Impurity on the ground*:

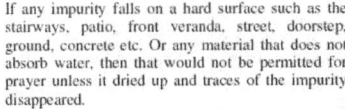

If any impurity falls on a hard surface such as the stairways, patio, front veranda, street, doorstep, ground, concrete etc. Or any material that does not absorb water, then that would not be permitted for prayer unless it dried up and traces of the impurity disappeared.

Method of cleaning: to pour water over the area until one is reasonably sure it has been washed away.

- al-Marghinani, *al-Hidayah*, p.155:

إن أصابت الأرض نجاسة فجفت بالشمس وذهب أثرها جازت الصلاة على مكانها

"[...] If the earth has impurity on it and dries up in the sun such that traces of the impurity disappear, then prayer on that surface would be permitted [...]"

Some Basic Application
of *Fiqh* Principles – *Shiny Surfaces*

Scenario A: *Impurity on shiny surfaces*:

> If any impurity falls on a shiny surface like a mirror, tile, ceramic, glass, fibre glass, etc. Then the surface will be impure to pray on it.
>
> **Method of purifying**: to purify it, it is sufficient to merely wipe over the surface until t he impurity disappears; pouring water over will also suffice should one want to.

- In al-Marghinani's *al-Hidayah*, 1:51 it states:

والنجاسة إذا أصابت المرآة أو السيف اكتفى بمسحهما ، بما يزول به أثرها ومثلهما كل نقيل لا مسام له كزجاح وعظم وآنية مدهونة وظفر لأنه لا يداخله النجاسة وما على ظاهره يزول بالمسح

"[...] (if impurities fall on a surface such as a mirror or a sword, it is sufficient to just wipe the impurity off) because by doing that the traces disappear; this is the case for any surface that does not have pores like glass [...]"

- The *Hashiyah* of Imam al-Tahtawi on al-Shurunbulali's *Maraqi al-Falah*, 1:190:

إلا في المني فإنه يطهر بالفرك قوله : ونحوه من كل صقيل لا مسام له

"Except for semen which is purified by scraping it off [s: when it is dry] which is the case for every material that does not have pores [...]"

Some Basic Application
of *Fiqh* Principles – *Mani*

Scenario A: *Impurity on clothes:*

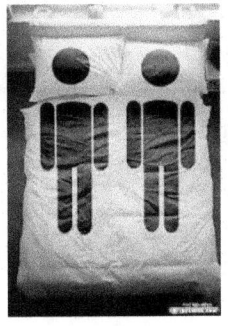

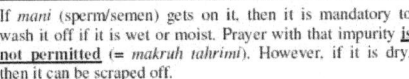

> If *mani* (sperm/semen) gets on it, then it is mandatory to wash it off if it is wet or moist. Prayer with that impurity <u>is not permitted</u> (= *makruh tahrimi*). However, if it is dry, then it can be scraped off.
>
> <u>Method of purifying</u>: washing the area of the impurity three times with a tight squeeze/rinse between each wash if it is wet or moist; if it is dry then it can be scraped off the area it has dried up on.

- In *al-Fatawa al-Hindiyyah*, 1:44:

الْمَنِيُّ إذَا أَصَابَ الثَّوْب فَإِنْ كَان رَطْبًا يَجِبُ غَسْلُهُ وَإِنْ جفّ عَلى الثَّوْب أَجْزَأ فِيه الْفِرَّكُ

"[...] and if semen falls on clothes then if it is moist or wet, then it is mandatory to wash it; if it is dry, then it is sufficient to scrape it off [...]"

- The *Hashiyah* of Imam al-Tahtawi on al-Shurunbulali's *Maraqi al-Falah*, 1:190:

إلا في المَني فَإنه بطهر بالفرك قوله : ونحوود من كل صقيل لا مسام له

"Except for semen which is purified by scraping it off [s: when it is dry] which is the case for every material that does not have pores [...]"

Some Basic Application
of *Fiqh* Principles – *Madhi* and *Wadi*

Scenario A: *Impurity on clothes*:

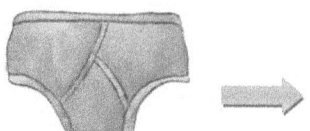

If *madhi* (pre-seminal fluid) or *wadi* (post-seminal discharge) gets on it, then if it is less than the diameter of 2.75 cm, the prayer with that amount of impurity (*najasah*) will be valid but disliked (*makruh tanzihi*). If it is more than 2.75cm, then prayer with that amount of impurity **is not permitted** (= *makruh tahrimi*).

Method of purifying: washing the area of the clothes **three times** and then squeezing it. It is not enough to let the *madhi* and *wadi* just dry up.

The same ruling will apply if they were to fall on the body, i.e. the area is just washed.

- al-Shurunbulali, *Maraqi al-Falah*, p.155:

"وما بنقض الوضوء بخروجه من بدن الإنسان" كالدم السائل والمني والمذي والودي والاستحاضة والحيض والنفاس والقيء ملء الفم ونجاستها غليظة بالاتفاق لعدم معارض دليل لنجاستها عنده ولعدم مساغ الاجتهاد في طهارتها عدها

"[...] and *wudu'* is broken with whatever exists the human body like flowing blood, sperm (*mani*), pre-seminal fluid (*madhi*), post-seminal discharge (*wadi*) chronic bleeding, menstruation, post-birth bleeding [...]"

- The *Hashiyah* of Imam al-Tahtawi on al-Shurunbulali's *Maraqi al-Falah*, p.156:

"وعفي قدر الدرهم" أي عفا الشارع عن ذلك والمراد عفا عن الفساد به وإلا فكراهة التحريم باقية إجماعا إن بلغت الدرهم ونزيها إن لم تبلغ

"What is meant by 'the amount of a dirham is excused' is that the Prayer will not be invalidated if it were to be on the clothes [...]"

§8. *Istinja'* – washing the private Parts

- Everyone answers the call of nature.

- The blessed Prophet has even shown his *umma* the details pertaining to the mode and manner of defecating and relieving h/herself.

- Linguistically, *'intinja"* (الإستنجاء) refers to washing or wiping the area where excrement is discharged from (i.e. the bowels). In legal (*shar`i*) terms, it refers to removing filth with water and the like.[75]

- *Istinja'*[76] is of three types:

  [1] *sunna* when the filth that exits the area has not spread beyond the boundary of its outlet (*al-makhraj*), e.g. when excrement does not smear beyond the perimeter of the anus.[77]

  [2] *wajib* when the filth does exit the area and spreads beyond the boundary of its outlet being the size approximately of a dirham. Thus water (or any liquid cleanser) will have to be used.[78]

  [3] *fard* when the filth does exit the area and spreads beyond the boundary of its outlet being **more than** the size approximately of a dirham. Thus water (or any liquid cleanser) will have to be used.[79]

---

[75] Wahba, *Sabil al-Falah*, p.19, n.2.
[76] See al-Quduri, *Mukhtasar*, p.2 (= *al-Lubab* of al-Maydani, 1:70) and al-Marghinani, *al-Hidaya*, 1:39-40 (= English trans. 1:75-77).
[77] al-Shurunbulali, *Maraqi al-Falah*, 1:75.
[78] al-Shurunbulali, *Nur al-Idah*, p.31 and idem, *Maraqi al-Sa`adat*, p.66.
[79] al-Shurunbulali, *Nur al-Idah*, p.31 and idem, *Maraqi al-Sa`adat*, p.66.

- Some of the emphasised *sunna* aspects of *istinja'* include:

  1. To use cleans stones or anything like it, as long as it is not

     a. Edible (food, fruits),
     b. Harmful (glass),
     c. Impure (dung, bone) or
     d. Valuable (fabrics, silks).[80]

  2. To purify the whole area.[81]

  3. It is recommended (*mandub*) to use three stones (and the like) even if the area is cleaned with less.[82]

  4. It is recommended to enter with the left foot and exit with the right foot seeking refuge from Satan and protection from Allah.[83]

- Some of the etiquettes (*adab*) of *istinja'* include:

  1. To seek a place as far as possible so people cannot hear, see or smell anything.[84]

  2. To choose an appropriate place so no splashes or smatterings fall on one's clothes.[85]

  3. Removing jewellery (e.g. rings), religious inscriptions, etc. before entering the toilet.[86]

---

[80] al-Shurunbulali, *Nur al-Idah*, p.31 and idem, *Maraqi al-Sa'adat*, p.66.
[81] al-Shurunbulali, *Nur al-Idah*, p.31 and idem, *Maraqi al-Sa'adat*, p.66.
[82] Ibn 'Abidin, *Radd al-Muhtar*, 1:225.
[83] Abu Dawud, *Sunan* (#4-5 & 28).
[84] Abu Dawud, *Sunan* (#1).
[85] Abu Dawud, *Sunan* (#3).
[86] Abu Dawud, *Sunan* (#18).

4. To sit leaning/tilting on one's left side.[87]

- Some of the undesirables (*makruhat*) of *istinja'* include:

    1. To unbutton before going to the toilet.[88]

    2. To talk to another person unless there is a real need.[89]

    3. To face the sun or the moon directly while relieving oneself.[90]

    4. To relieve oneself while facing a blowing wind (as it affects others).

    5. To urinate in the bathtub or shower (which includes drains).[91]

    6. To urinate in hollows, potholes, holes, etc. as jinn or other creatures may reside there.[92]

    7. To urinate/defecate in streets, thoroughfares.[93]

    8. To urinate/defecate in flowing water.

    9. To urinate/defecate in stagnant water.[94]

    10. To urinate/defecate in shaded areas.[95]

---

[87] Abu Dawud, *Sunan* (#15).
[88] Nasa'i, *Sunan* (#14).
[89] Abu Dawud, *Sunan* (#14)
[90] Because both are magnificent signs of Allah. See Ibn `Abidin, *Radd al-Muhtar*, 1:228.
[91] Nasa'i, *Sunan* (#21).
[92] Nasa'i, *Sunan* (#34).
[93] Ibn Majah, *Sunan* (#325).
[94] Ibn Majah, *Sunan* (#338).

11. To relieve oneself under a fruit tree.[96]

12. To urinate while standing unless there is a real need.[97]

13. To use one's right hand.[98]

14. Using anything of value (e.g. silk, cotton, etc.).

15. To face the *qibla*.[99]

16. To remember the names of Allah.[100]

17. To reply to any greetings (*al-salam*).[101]

18. Failing to wash one's hand after relieving oneself.[102]

19. Failing to be considerate to others (e.g. cleaning the toilet, leaving enough water, etc.).[103]

- Some of the prohibitions of *istinja'* include:

  1. To relieve oneself in front of others (includes public cubicles).

---

[95] al-Shurunbulali, *Nur al-Idah*, p.35.

[96] al-Shurunbulali, *Nur al-Idah*, p.35.

[97] Ibn Majah, *Sunan* (#303).

[98] Abu Dawud, *Sunan* (#29).

[99] Muslim, *Sahih* (#388). This is prohibitively disliked (*makruh tahriman*). See Ibn `Abidin, *Radd al-Muhtar*, 1:228.

[100] Abu Dawud, *Sunan* (#16).

[101] Ibn Majah, *Sunan* (#346).

[102] Abu Dawud, *Sunan* (#41).

[103] Muslim, *Sahih* (#398).

2. To use objects that is unlawful for that purpose (like expensive materials).

- *Istibra'* (الإستبراء): this is a procedure of cleaning residual urine drops or impurities related to when men urinate. Drops of urine remain in the urethra after men relieve themselves and hence by doing the following, the urinary tract maybe fully emptied:[104]

1. rubbing or rolling the penis several times with the thumb and index fingers,
2. hopping on one leg,
3. coughing,
4. walking around,
5. lying down or
6. slightly squeezing the penis[105].

---

[104] Ibn `Abidin, *Radd al-Muhtar*, 1:230 and 1:344-245:

قَوْلُهُ: يَجِبُ الِاسْتِبْرَاءُ إلَخْ) هُوَ طَلَبُ الْبَرَاءَةِ مِنْ الْخَارِجِ بِشَيْءٍ مِمَّا ذَكَرَهُ الشَّارِحُ حَتَّى يَسْتَيْقِنَ بِزَوَالِ الْأَثَرِ... وَلِذَا قَالَ الشُّرُنْبُلَالِيُّ: يَلْزَمُ الرَّجُلَ الِاسْتِبْرَاءُ حَتَّى يَزُولَ أَثَرُ الْبَوْلِ وَيَطْمَئِنَّ قَلْبُهُ. وَقَالَ: عَبَّرْت بِاللُّزُومِ لِكَوْنِهِ أَقْوَى مِنْ الْوَاجِبِ؛ لِأَنَّ هَذَا يُفَوِّتُ الْجَوَازَ لِفَوْتِهِ فَلَا يَصِحُّ لَهُ الشُّرُوعُ فِي الْوُضُوءِ حَتَّى يَطْمَئِنَّ بِزَوَالِ الرَّشْحِ

al-Fatawa al-Hindiyya, 1:54:

والاستبراء واجب حتى يستقر قلبه على انقطاع العود كذا في الظهيرية قال بعضهم: يستنجي بعدما يخطو خطوات وقال بعضهم: يركض برجله على الأرض ويتنحنح ويلف رجله اليمنى على اليسرى وينزل من الصعود إلى الهبوط والصحيح أن طباع الناس مختلفة فمتى وقع في قلبه أنه تم استفراغ ما في السبيل يستنجي هكذا في شرح منية المصلي لابن أمير الحاج والمضمرات

[105] Ibn Majah, *Sunan* (#321).

§9. Miscellaneous Injunctions

1. **Urinals**: urinating in public places that have urinals leaves one to expose the `awra in front of others. This is not permitted.

2. **Toilet paper**: there is no harm in using toilet paper as it is produced for the purpose of cleaning although it is better to use both paper and water.

3. **Dogs**: only the saliva of a dog is impure and according to the strongest Hanafi position its skin and hair is **not** impure.

4. **Washing machines**: Using washing machines is permitted as long as there are three separate cycles of washing with entry of fresh water each time. It is better to remove the impurity off the item of clothing first with water before putting it into the machine.

5. **Using detergents**: using soaps, detergent powders, washing liquids etc. does not affect the unconditioned/absolute (*mutlaq*) status of water and hence can be used to remove filth but not for ritual purification purposes (i.e. *wudu'* or *ghusl*).

SECTION 2: *WUDU'*
('RITUAL ABLUTION')

———— ♦ ————

§1. Preliminaries of *Wudu'*

- Imam Tirmidhi in his *Sunan* mentions the following narration:

"From Abu Hayya (Allah be pleased with him) who said: 'I saw `Ali perform the ritual ablution (*wudu'*) and he did the following':

[1] Washed his hands up to the wrists. [2] Then he rinsed his mouth three times. [3] And he drew water into his nostrils three times and flushed it out. [4] He washed his face three times. [5] He then washed his arms three times [6] and thereafter he wiped his head once. [7] And then he washed his feet up to the ankles. [8] He then stood up and drank from the remaining water saying: 'I wanted to show you how the Messenger of Allah (Allah bless him and grant him peace) used to purify himself'..."[106]

رأيت عليا توضأ فغسل كفيه حتى أنقاهما ثم تمضمض ثلاثا واستنشق ثلاثا وغسل وجهه ثلاثا وغسل ذراعيه ثلاثا ثم مسح برأسه ثم غسل قدميه إلى الكعبين ثم قام فأخذ فضل طهوره فشرب وهو قائم ثم قال أحببت أن أريكم كيف طهور النبي صلى الله عليه وسلم.

---

[106] Narrated by Tirmidhi in his *Sunan* (#45 and 48) and Nasa'i in his *Sunan* (#95-96). See also al-Diya' al-Maqdisi in *al-Mukhtar*, 2:409 (#795) and Imam Ahmad in his *Musnad*, 1/127 (#1046); Abu Ya`la in his *Musnad*, 1:385 and al-Bahlawi, *Adillat al-Hanafiyy*a, p.32 (#11).

- The primary text used as a basis for this section is the primer on Hanafi devotional injunctions entitled *Nur al-Idah* ('The Light of Clarification') by the regional Qadi of Egypt Imam al-Shurunbulali with his own interlinear commentary of the manual entitled *Maraqi al-Falah* ('The Ascent to Felicity').

§2. The definition of *wudu'*

- *Wudu'* is defined as: "Washing the face, hands and feet and wiping the head."[107]

- Other words for *wudu'* include 'tahara' ('purification') as used in the books of *fiqh* and 'tuhur' (as mentioned in the *hadith* above).

- The word *wudu'* also refers to just washing the face and hands as mentioned by Sayyiduna Mu`adh ibn Jabal and Ibn Mas`ud (Allah be pleased with them both):

"From Mu`adh ibn Jabal who said: we would call washing the hands and mouth '*wudu*'' but not the *wudu'* that is obligatory..."[108]

عن معاذ ابن جبل قال: كن نسمي غسل اليد و الفم وضوءا و ليس بواجب.

"From ibn Mas`ud that he washed his hand and wiped his face after eating and then said: 'this is the '*wudu*'' of one who is already with a valid *wudu*'...'"[109]

عن ابن مسعود انه غسل يده من طعام ثم مسح وجهه و قال هذا وضوء من لم يحدث.

- The Arabic word *wudu'* / وضوء is pronounced differently with each different vowelling giving a different meaning:

[1] *wadu'* means water used for ablution;

---

[107] See M. Wahba, *Sabil al-Falah Sharh Nur al-Idah*, p.26 f.
[108] See the *Sunan* of Imam al-Bayhaqi, 1:141.
[109] Nasa'i, *Sunan* (#130).

[2] *widu'* means the vessel that contains water for ablution and

[3] *wudu'* means to perform ablution.[110]

---

[110] Madani, *The Book of Purification*, p.165.

§3. The virtues of *wudu'*

- There are innumerable narrations (*ahadith*) that mention the virtues (*fada'il*) and excellence of *wudu'* such as:

[1] Allah raises the rank of those who perform it in honour, status and reward:

From Abu Hurayra: The Messenger of Allah said: **"'Shall I suggest to you that by which Allah will obliterate the sins and elevate the ranks?'** The Companions replied: 'Yes, Messenger of Allah'. **'Perform the *wudu'* completely even against all difficulty'** [...]".[111]

ألا أدلكم على ما يمحو الله به الخطايا ويرفع به الدرجات ؟ "قالوا : بلى. يا رسول الله ! قال " إسباغ الوضوء على المكاره. وكثرة الخطا إلى المساجد. وانتظار الصلاة بعد الصلاة. فذلكم الرباط". وليس في حديث شعبة ذكر الرباط. وفي حديث مالك ثنتين" فذلكم الرباط. فذلكم الرباط.

[2] Allah forgives sins through *wudu'*:

"From Sayyiduna ʿUthman Ibn ʿAffan: "Whoever performs *wudu'* and performs it properly, all his sins fall from away from his body. The sins will even fall from his finger nails."[112]

من توضأ فأحسن الوضوء خرجت خطاياه من جسده . حتى تخرج من تحت أظفاره.

---

[111] Muslim, *Sahih* (#251).
[112] Muslim, *Sahih* (#361).

[3] *Wudu'* is a sign of *iman* ('belief'):

From Abu Malik al-Ash`ari: "Performing *wudu'* properly is part of true belief [...]".[113]

إسباغ الوضوء شطر الإيمان...

[4] *Wudu'* protects from Shaytan's traps:

From Abu Hurayra: "The Messenger of Allah (Allah bless him and grant him peace) said: '**when one of you sleeps, the devil ties three knots at the back of his head saying with each knot, you have a long night so rest and sleep. He wakes up remembering Allah he unties one knot; if he performs *wudu'* he unties another knot**' [...]".[114]

أن رسول الله صلى الله عليه وسلم قال :

يعقد الشيطان على قافية رأس أحدكم إذا

هو نام ثلاث عقد، يضرب كل عقدة

مكانها : عليك ليل طويل فارقد، فإن

استيقظ فذكر الله انحلت عقدة، فإن

توضأ انحلت عقدة، فإن صلى انحلت

عقده كلها، فأصبح نشيطا طيب النفس ،

وإلا أصبح خبيث النفس كسلان...

---

[113] Ibn Majah, *Sunan* (#229) as part of a longer *hadith*.
[114] Bukhari, *Sahih* (#3269).

§4. Some outlines regarding *Wudu'*

- *Wudu'* is performed in order to make lawful certain other actions, e.g. the Prayer (*al-salah*), otherwise they cannot be performed.[115] This is known as the *sabab* ('reason') for *wudu'*.

- *Wudu'* only applies to the present and temporal world although its performance will accrue reward (*al-thawab*) in the Hereafter.[116]

- *Wudu'* is made obligatory due to 8 conditions:

  1. Being Muslim (*al-islam*).

  2. Being sane (*al-`aql*).

  3. Being mature (*al-bulugh*).

  4. The presence of sufficient amount of water (so that the required body parts can be washed).

  5. Being in a state of minor ritual purity (*hadath*), e.g. having gone to the toilet, breaking wind, flowing blood, etc.

  6. Not being on the menstrual cycle/period (*al-hayd*).

  7. Not being in a state of post-birth bleeding (*al-nifas*).

  8. Restricted time limit (*diq al-waqt*).[117]

---

[115] al-Shurunbulali, *Nur al-Idah*, p.37.
[116] al-Shurunbulali, *Nur al-Idah*, p.37.
[117] al-Shurunbulali, *Nur al-Idah*, pp.37-38.

- *Wudu'* is of three general types or categories and they are:[118]

[1] *Fard* (obligatory):

1. When performing any prayer which includes the funeral prayer [*salat al-janaza*]).
2. When doing the prostration of recital (*sajidat al-tilawa*).
3. When touching the Qur'an (even one verse).

[2] *Wajib* (necessary):

1. When performing *tawaf* around the Ka`ba.

[3] *Mandub* (recommended):

1. Before going to sleep and waking up from sleep.
2. To refresh the *wudu'*.
3. After backbiting, lying, slandering, etc.
4. After every mistake and wrongdoing.
5. After listening to evil poetry/contents.
6. When laughing extremely loudly outside of prayer.
7. After washing a dead body or carrying it.
8. Performing *wudu'* at each prayer time.
9. Before *ghusl* (the bath).
10. To perform *wudu'* in between sexual intercourses.
11. When one is in a state of anger.
12. When wishing to recite the Qur'an.
13. When reading/narrating/studying *hadith* or any books of *fiqh*, *tafsir*, etc.
14. When doing the *adhan*, *iqama* and *khutba*.
15. When visiting the tomb of the Prophet.
16. When standing at `Arafa and when running between Safa and Marwa.

---

[118] al-Shurunbulali, *Nur al-Idah*, pp.46-49.

17. After eating camel meat.
18. When the noble scholars have real disagreement (*ikhtilaf*) over a particular issue.[119]

- The Hanafi scholars consider it recommended and rewardable to renew the *wudu'* or perform it after any action where the Imams differed over, e.g. when touching a woman, or when touching the private parts, or when eating camel meat, etc. in the hope of benefitting from the complete reward and benefits of all understandings.[120]

---

[119] For an extensive discussion with evidences on this particular *mas'ala* ('legal question'), see Mufti Abdul Wajid Qadiri, *Fatawa Europe*, pp.121-127.
[120] al-Shurunbulali, *Maraqi al-Falah*, p.35.

§5. That which makes *Wudu'* Valid

- At least three matters make *wudu'* valid and acceptable otherwise it will be invalid:

    1. Water must reach the outer skin and hence any area required to be washed must not remain dry.

    2. Anything that is incompatible with the *wudu'* such as menstruation/period, post-birth bleeding, being in a state of minor ritual impurity, etc.

    3. The removal of any object or barrier that prevents water reaching the skin, e.g. solids, wax, adhesives, films, skin barriers, etc.[121]

---

[121] al-Shurunbulali, *Maraqi al-Falah*, p.63:

(ما) أي شيء (يمنع الماء) أن يصل إلى الجسد (كعجين) وشمع ورمص بخارج العين بتغميضها (وجب) أي

افترض (غسل ما تحته) بعد إزالة المانع

§6. The Obligatory Aspects of *Wudu'*

- Allah mentions in the Qur'an al-Karim 5:6:

يَا أَيُّهَا الَّذِينَ آمَنُوا إِذَا قُمْتُمْ إِلَى الصَّلَاةِ فَاغْسِلُوا وُجُوهَكُمْ وَأَيْدِيَكُمْ إِلَى الْمَرَافِقِ وَامْسَحُوا بِرُءُوسِكُمْ وَأَرْجُلَكُمْ إِلَى الْكَعْبَيْنِ ۩

{O you who believe! when you rise up to perform the prayer, wash your faces and wash your hands as far as the elbows and wipe your heads and wash your feet to the ankles...}

- al-Shurunbulali mentions in *Nur al-Idah*:

"The pillars (*arkan*) of *wudu'* are four in number and its obligatory features are: [1] The first is to wash the face and its limit lengthwise is from the top of the forehead to the bottom of the chin and breadth wise its length is from one earlobe to the other. [2] The second is washing the arms with the elbows at least once. [3] The third is washing the feet with the ankles and [4] The fourth is wiping over quarter of the head."[122]

أركان الوضوء أربعة وهي فرائضه: الأول

غسل الوجه وحده طولا من مبدأ سطح

الجبهة إلى أسفل الذقن وحده عرضا ما

بين شحمتا الأذنين و الثاني غسل يديه مع

مرفقيه و الثالث غسل رجليه مع كعبيه و

الرابع مسح ربع رأسه.

---

[122] al-Shurunbulali, *Nur al-Idah*, pp.36-37 and idem, *Maraqi al-Sa`adat*, pp.41-43. cf. also al-Quduri, *Mukhtasar*, p.2 (= *al-Lubab* of al-Maydani, 1:31-32) and al-Marghinani, *al-Hidaya*, 1:12-13 (= English trans. 1:7-10).

- The obligatory (*fard*) aspects of *wudu'* therefore are four:[123]

[1] Washing[124] the hands (including the wrists and the elbows).

[2] Washing the face (which does not include the eye ball).

[3] Wiping the head (at least a quarter [*rub' al-ra's*]).

[4] Washing the feet (including the ankles).

- If these four parts of the body are washed – even in no particular order – at least once such that not even a hair on those parts remains dry (e.g. whether by rain, falling in the water, swimming, dipping into a river, etc.) then *wudu'* will technically be valid.

---

[123] See Alahazrat Imam Ahmad Reza Khan, *al-Jud al-Huluw fi Arkan al-Wudu'*, pp.264-281 and *Khulasat Tibyan al-Wudu'*, pp.599-602 for a detailed discussion on the Hanafi particulars. See also Ibn 'Abidin, *Radd al-Muhtar*, 1:66; al-Haskafi, *Durr al-Mukhtar*, 1:19 and Ibn al-Nujaym, *Bahr al-Ra'iq*, 1:11.

[124] Imam 'Abd al-Ghani al-Nablusi writes:

"...and the term 'washing' (*al-ghasl*) means: pouring water. And the determined measure of washing with water is for water to drip even if it is one drop according to Abu Hanifa and Muhammad al-Shaybani whereas for Abu Yusuf it is sufficient that someone just pour water on any part of the body even if it does not drip as mentioned in *Fath al-Qadir*. In *al-Fayd* it mentions that the minimum is that two drops of water flow [s: off the body] and this is the most correct opinion." See *al-Lubab*, 1:32.

والغسل : إسالة الماء : وحد الإسالة في الغسل :

أن يتقاطر الماء ولو قطرة عندهما وعند أبي يوسف

يجزئ إذا سال على العضو وإن لم يقطر فتح وفي

الفيض : أقله قطرتان في الأصح إ. ه

- There are no necessary aspects to perform (*wajib* `*amali*) in *wudu'* (and *ghusl*) as mentioned in the *fiqh* manuals:

"Our scholars are in full agreement that there are no necessary (*wajib*) aspects to *wudu'*..."[125]

إتفق أصحابنا انه لا واجب في الوضوء...

"And it is the case that there are no necessary (*wajib*) aspects to *wudu'* nor are there necessary (*wajib*) aspects to the *ghusl*..."[126]

أفاد انه لا واجب للوضوء و لا للغسل...

---

[125] Ibn al-Nujaym, *al-Bahr al-Ra'iq*, 1:11.
[126] Ibn `Abidin, *Radd al-Muhtar*, 1:20.

§7. The *Sunna* Aspects of *Wudu'*

- al-Shurunbulali states in *Nur al-Idah*:

"There are eighteen *sunna* aspects to the *wudu'*: [1] washing the hands up to the wrists. [2] To begin with the 'bismillah'. [3] Using the *siwak* at the beginning even if it is with the fingers when one does not have a *siwak*. [4] Rinsing the mouth three times even of one makes three rinses with one scoop of water. [5] Running water in the nostrils three times and with three separate scoops. [6] To increase the depth of rinsing the mouth [s: e.g. to gargle the water] and nostrils [s: e.g. to snuff the water]. [7] To pass fingers through the bottom of a large beard with water in the palm of the hand. [8] To interlace the fingers. [9] To wash the body parts three times. [10] To wipe the entire head once. [11] Wiping the ears even if it is with the water used to wipe the head. [12] Rubbing the body parts with water (*al-dalk*). [13] Washing the body parts successively [s: without stopping to let the parts dry]. [14] Intention (*niyya*). [15] Washing the body parts in the sequence shown by Allah

يسن في الوضوء ثمانية عشر شيئا : غسل اليدين إلى الرسغين والتسمية ابتداء والسواك في ابتدائه ولو بالأصبع عند فقده والمضمضة ثلاثا ولو بغرفة والاستنشاق بثلاث غرفات و المبالغة في المضمضة و الاستنشاق و تخليل اللحية الكثة بكف ماء من أسفلها و تخليل الأصابع و تثليث الغسل و استيعاب الرأس بالمسح مرة و مسح الأذنين ولو بماء الرأس و الدلك و الولاء و النية و الترتيب كما نص الله تعالى في كتابه و البداءة بالميامن و رؤوس الأصابع و مقدم الرأس و مسح الرقبة لا الحلقوم وقيل إن الأربعة الأخيرة مستحبة.

in His Book. [16] Beginning from the right. [17] Beginning from the tips of the fingers and toes and beginning from the front part of the head [s: when wiping it]. [18] To wipe the neck and not the throat. It is mentioned that these last four points are not *sunna* but recommended or desirable actions (*mustahabb*)."[127]

- Thus, the Prophetic *sunna*[128] of *wudu'* are 14 with 4 additional desirable and recommended (*mustahabb*) actions according to one Hanafi position:

  1. Making the intention (*al-niyya*).[129]

  2. Reciting the 'basmalah' (*bismillahir rahmanir rahim*).[130]

  3. Washing the hands three times.[131]

---

[127] al-Shurunbulali, *Nur al-Idah*, pp.40-43. See also al-Quduri, *Mukhtasar*, pp.2-3 (= *al-Lubab* of al-Maydani, 1:33-35) and al-Marghinani, *al-Hidaya*, 1:13-14 (= English trans. 1:10-14).

[128] Imam al-Nablusi writes:

"Linguistically, the term 'sunna' means 'a path' whether acceptable or non-acceptable and its plural is 'sunan'. The *shar'i* meaning is: everything the Prophet (Allah bless him and grant him peace) continuously did and only missed once or sometimes." See *al-Lubab*, 1:33.

جمع سنة وهي لغة : الطريقة مرضية كانت أو

غير مرضية وفي الشريعة : ما واظب عليه النبي

صلى الله عليه وسلم مع الترك أحيانا...

[129] Bukhari, *Sahih* (#1).

[130] al-Haythami, *Majma' al-Zawa'id*, 1:220.

4. To rinse the mouth three times (*al-madmada*).[132]

5. To rinse the nose three times (*al-istinshaq*).[133]

6. To rinse thoroughly the mouth and nose three times (*al-mubalagha fi'l-madmada wa 'l-istinshaq*).

7. To wash all the required body parts three times (*al-tathlith*).[134]

8. Using the *miswak/siwak.*[135]

9. Running fingers through the beard (*al-khilal*).[136]

10. Running fingers through the fingers and toes.[137]

11. Wiping over the entire head once (*mash al-ra's*).[138]

12. Wiping the ears simultaneously (*mash al-uthanayn*).[139]

13. Rubbing the required body parts (*al-dalk*).[140]

---

[131] Nasa'i, *Sunan* (#94).

[132] Abu Dawud, *Sunan* (#123).

[133] Bukhari, *Sahih* (#3052).

[134] Bukhari, *Sahih* (#331).

[135] For more on the rewards of using the *miswak* and a discussion, see Mulla `Ali al-Qari, *Mirqat al-Mafatih*, 2:3 f.

[136] Tirmidhi, *Sunan* (#28).

[137] Tirmidhi, *Sunan* (#718).

[138] Bukhari, *Sahih* (#179).

[139] Tirmidhi, *Sunan* (#32).

[140] al-Hakim, *al-Mustadrak*, 1:243.

14. Successively washing the required body parts before the dry up.

The desirables include:

15. To begin from the tips of the fingers and toes.

16. Following the proper sequence (*al-tartib*).

17. Beginning from the right side (*bada'a bi 'l-mayamin*).[141]

18. Wiping the nape of the neck and not the throat.[142]

---

[141] Ibn Majah, *Sunan* (#369).
[142] Ibn Hajar al-`Asqalani, *Talkhis al-Habir*, 1:93.

§8. The *Adab* Aspects of *Wudu'*

- al-Shurunbulali lists the etiquettes (*adab*) in *Nur al-Idah*:

"And the desired aspects of *wudu'* are fourteen in number: [1] To sit on a raised place. [2] Facing the direction of the Ka`ba (*al-qibla*). [3] Not seeking help from others in performing the *wudu'*. [4] Abstaining from talking in a way that people generally talk. [5] To combine the intention in the heart with verbal utterances of the tongue. [6] To recite the various supplications (*al-du`a'*) that have been transmitted down. [7] To say, '*bismillahir rahmanir rahim*' when washing every required body part. [8] To insert the little finger into the opening of the ears. [9] To move the wide and loose ring around the finger. [10] To one rinse the mouth and then two to draw water into the nostrils with the right hand and withdraw the nasal mucus with the left hand. [11] Performing *wudu'* before the time of the Prayer enters except for someone who is exempt (*al-ma`dhur*). [12] To recite the *shahadatayn* ('the two declarations of

من آداب الوضوء أربعة عشر شيئا الجلوس في مكان مرتفع واستقبال القبلة وعدم الاستعانة بغيره وعدم التكلم بكلام الناس والجمع بين نية القلب وفعل اللسان والدعاء بالمأثور والتسمية عند كل عضو وإدخال خنصره في صماخ أذنيه وتحريك خاتمه الواسع والمضمضة والاستنشاق باليد اليمنى والامتخاط باليسرى والتوضؤ قبل دخول الوقت لغير المعذور والإتيان بالشهادتين بعده وأن يشرب من فضل الوضوء قائما وأن يقول اللهم اجعلني من التوابين و اجعلني من المتطهرين.

faith'). [13] To drink the remaining water of *wudu'* standing up. [14] To recite: 'O Allah! Make me from those who repent and make me from those who are pure'."[143]

- Therefore, there are 14 practices that are considered *adab*[144] related to the *wudu'*:

1. Sitting on an elevated place.

2. Facing the Qibla (*istiqbal al-qibla*).

3. Performing *wudu'* without assistance.

4. Refrain from talking.

---

[143] al-Shurunbulali, *Nur al-Idah*, pp.43-45. See also al-Quduri, *Mukhtasar*, p.3 (= *al-Lubab* of al-Maydani, 1:36).

[144] Imam 'Abd al-Ghani al-Nablusi writes:

"...Linguistically, the term 'mustahabb' means 'something desirable'. Customarily, it is said to refer to that which the Prophet (Allah bless him and grant him peace) did once but did not do another time. The word 'mandub' is said to be what the Prophet performed once or twice. It is also said that *mustahabb* and *mandub* mean the same thing and this is the position of the scholars of *usul al-fiqh*. It is mentioned in *al-Tahrir*: 'and the *mandub* and the *mustahabb* are those things that he [s: meaning the Prophet] did not persist in doing although he did not do it after having desired to do it.'" See *al-Lubab*, 1:36.

المستحب لغة : هو الشيء المحبوب وعرفا قيل

: هو ما فعله النبي صلى الله عليه وسلم مرة وتركه

أخرى والمندوب : ما فعله مرة أو مرتين وقيل :

هما سواء وعليه الأصوليون قال في التحرير : وما

لم يواظب عليه مندوب ومستحب وإن لم يفعله

بعدما رغب فيه إ. ه

5. Combining the intention in the heart and the words.

6. To make the relevant *du`as*.[145]

7. To recite the 'basmalah' when washing each part.

8. To insert the little finger in the ear opening.

9. To move the loose ring around (*tahrik khatimat al-wasi`*).

10. To gargle and draw water into the nostrils with the right hand and flush it out with the left.

11. Performing *wudu'* before the time of prayer.

12. To recite the two *shahada*.

13. To drink from the remaining water of *wudu'*.[146]

14. To recite the *du`a'*: O Allah! Make me from those who repent and make me from those who are pure'.

---

[145] Muslim, *Sahih* (#122) and al-Hakim, *al-Mustadrak*, 1:752.
[146] Nasa'i, *Sunan* (#94) and Ibn Khuzayma, *Sahih*, 1:11.

§9. That which is disliked in *Wudu'*

- al-Shurunbulali states the disliked aspects of *wudu'* in *Nur al-Idah*:

"There are six matters disliked for the one performing *wudu'*: [1] wasting water. [2] Using very little water. [3] To slap water on the face. [4] To speak to anyone. [5] To seek help from another person without a reason or need. [6] To wipe the head three times using new water each time."[147]

ويكره للمتوضىء ستة أشياء الإسراف في الماء والتقتير فيه و ضرب الوجه به والتكلم بكلام الناس والاستعانة بغيره من غير عذر وتثليث المسح بماء جديد.

- Thus from the above we have the following disliked aspects of *wudu'*:

1. Wasting water.

2. Using too little water.

3. To slap water on the face.

4. To unnecessarily speak to anyone.

5. To seek help to perform *wudu'* without a valid reason.

6. To wipe the head three times using new water each time.

---

[147] al-Shurunbulali, *Nur al-Idah*, pp.45-46.

- Although if one does commit these actions, the *wudu'* is not invalidated, nevertheless they should be avoided.

- Wasting water was cautioned against by the Messenger of Allah[148] and it means to use water – knowingly – beyond its need.[149]

---

[148] Ibn Majah, *Sunan* (#425) and Ahmad, *Musnad*, 2/221.

[149] Ibn `Abidin, *Radd al-Muhtar*, 1:132-133:

(قوله : والإسراف) أي بأن يستعمل منه فوق الحاجة الشرعية، لما أخرج ابن ماجه وغيره عن عبد الله بن عمرو بن العاص أن رسول الله صلى الله عليه وسلم مر بسعد وهو يتوضأ فقال : ما هذا السرف ؟ فقال : أفي الوضوء إسراف ؟ فقال : نعم، وإن كنت على نهر جار حلية (قوله : ومنه) أي من الإسراف الزيادة على الثلاث أي في الغسلات مع اعتقاد أن ذلك هو السنة لما قدمناه من الصحيح أن النهي محمول على ذلك، فإذا لم يعتقد ذلك وقصد الطمأنينة عند الشك، أو قصد الوضوء على الوضوء بعد الفراغ منه فلا كراهة كما مر تقريره (قوله : فيه) أي في الماء (قوله : تحريما إلخ) نقل ذلك في الحلية عن بعض المتأخرين من الشافعية وتبعه عليه في البحر وغيره، وهو مخالف لما قدمناه عن الفتح من عده ترك التقتير والإسراف من المندوبات، ومثله في البدائع وغيرها، لكن قال في الحلية : ذكر الحلواني أنه سنة؛ وعليه مشى قاضي خان، وهو وجيه ا ه واستوجبه في البحر أيضا وكذا في النهر . قال : والمراد بالسنة المؤكدة لإطلاق النهي عن الإسراف، وجعل في المنتقى الإسراف من المنهيات فتكون تحريمية لأن إطلاق الكراهة مصروف إلى التحريم، وبه يضعف جعله مندوبا .

أقول : قد تقدم أن النهي عنه في حديث: فمن زاد على هذا أو نقص فقد تعدى وظلم محمول على الاعتقاد عندنا، كما صرح به في الهداية وغيرها . وقال في البدائع : إنه الصحيح، حتى لو زاد أو نقص واعتقد أن الثلاث سنة لا يلحقه الوعيد وقدمنا أنه صريح في عدم كراهة ذلك يعني كراهة تحريم، فلا ينافي الكراهة التنزيهية، فما مشى عليه هنا في الفتح والبدائع وغيرهما من جعل تركه مندوبا مبني على ذلك التصحيح، فيكره تنزيها، ولا ينافيه عده من المنهيات كما عد منها لطم الوجه بالماء، فإن المكروه تنزيها منهي عنه حقيقة اصطلاحا، ومجازا لغة كما في التحرير . وأيضا فقد عده في الخزانة السمرقندية من المنهيات، لكن قيده بعدم اعتقاد تمام السنة بالثلاث، كما نقله الشيخ إسماعيل، وعليه يحمل قول من جعل تركه سنة، وليست الكراهة مصروفة إلى التحريم مطلقا كما ذكرناه آنفا، على أن الصارف للنهي عن التحريم ظاهر، فإن من أسرف في الوضوء بماء النهر مثلا مع عدم اعتقاد سنية ذلك نظير من ملأ إناء من النهر ثم أفرغه فيه، وليس في ذلك محذور سوى أنه عبث لا فائدة فيه، وهو في الوضوء زائد على المأمور به؛ فلذا سمي في الحديث إسرافا

قال في القاموس : الإسراف : التبذير أو ما أنفق في غير طاعة، ولا يلزم من كونه زائدا على المأمور به وغير طاعة أن يكون حراما، نعم إذا اعتقد سنيته يكون قد تعدى وظلم لاعتقاده ما ليس بقربة قربة، فلذا

- Washing the body parts have to be differentiated from wiping the body parts hence using a paucity of water is discouraged. Also, it is contrary to the *sunna* action.[150]

- Splashing water on the face or slapping it with water is contrary to the general dignity and honour given to the face.[151]

- One should also avoid talking while making *wudu'* as it distracts from its performance and distracts from making any relevant supplications.[152]

- Wiping the head several times is contrary to the *sunna* of wiping once and hence should be avoided.

- If one is able then one should perform *wudu'* without assistance. Imam al-Shurunbulali states:

"**(Seeking help from someone else)** based on what `Umar (Allah be pleased with him) said when he saw the Messenger of Allah (Allah bless him and grant him peace)

(الاستعانة بغيره) لقول عمر رضي الله عنه رأيت رسول الله صلى الله عليه وسلم يستقي ماء لوضوئه فبادرت أن أستقي له

حمل علماؤنا النهي على ذلك ، فحينئذ يكون منهيا عنه ويكون تركه سنة مؤكدة ، ويؤيده ما قدمه الشارح عن الجواهر من أن الإسراف في الماء الجاري جائز لأنه غير مضيع وقدمنا أن الجائز قد يطلق على ما لا يمتنع شرعا فيشمل المكروه تنزيها، وبهذا التقرير تتوافق عباراتهم . وأما ما ذكره الشارح هنا فقد علمت أنه ليس من كلام المشايخ المذهب فلا يعارض ما صرحوا به وصححوه، هذا ما ظهر لي في هذا المقام، والسلام. (قوله : فحرام) لأن الزيادة غير مأذون بها لأنه إنما يوقف ويساق لمن يتوضأ الوضوء الشرعي ولم يقصد إباحتها لغير ذلك حلية، وينبغي تقييده بما ليس بجار كالذي في صهريج أو حوض أو نحو إبريق، أما الجاري كماء مدارس دمشقوجوامعها فهو من المباح كماء النهر كما أفاده الرحمتي .

[150] al-Shurunbulali, *Maraqi al-Falah*, p.33.
[151] al-Shurunbulali, *Maraqi al-Falah*, p.33.
[152] al-Shurunbulali, *Maraqi al-Falah*, p.33.

pouring water for *wudu:'* I began to move so that I could help him where he said: 'stop o `Umar! I don't wish anyone to help me in my prayer'.[153] **(without a reason)** because necessity permits the prohibited and which is even more so in the case of when there is no prohibition. And Imam al-Wabri mentions how there is nothing wrong with this [s: i.e. someone helping in the *wudu'*] because a servant poured water on the Prophet (Allah bless him and grant him peace)[154] ,,[155]

فقال : "مه يا عمر فإني لا أريد أن يعينني

على صلاتي أحد" (من غير عذر) لأن

الضرورات تبيح المحظورات فكيف لما لا

حظر فيه وعن الإمام الوبري أنه لا بأس به

فإن الخادم كان يصب على النبي صلى

الله عليه وسلم...

---

[153] See al-Haythami, *Majma` al-Zawa'id*, 1:227.
[154] See for example Muslim, *Sahih* (#81 and 105); Abu Dawud, *Sunan* (#149); Ibn Majah, *Sunan* (#389); Malik, *al-Muwatta'* (#41) and Ahmad, *al-Musnad*, 4/249 and 251.
[155] al-Shurunbulali, *Maraqi al-Falah*, p.33 (the bold text is that of *Nur al-Idah*).

§10. That which Invalidates the *Wudu'*

- Allah states in the Qur'an al-Karim: {*or when any of you come when answering the call of nature [it is necessary to make wudu']*...}.[156]

- Generally, there are four main anatomical areas that are relevant for understanding the validity of *wudu'* and they have been discussed in depth by the noble *fuqaha'*.

- Below are scenarios where the *wudu'* is invalidated and hence will have to be renewed:[157]

Anatomical Areas

[1] **Penis/vagina**:

1. Urine
2. Blood.
3. Semen (*mani*) and pre-ejaculatory fluid (*madhi*).
4. Discharge

[2] **Anus**:

1. Excrement.
2. Wind.
3. Gas.
4. Discharge.

[3] **Mouth**:

1. Vomiting a mouthful of food.
2. Vomiting blood.

---

[156] Qur'an 5:6.
[157] See al-Shurunbulali, *Maraqi al-Falah*, pp.36-38; al-Quduri, al-*Mukhtasar*, pp.3-4 (= *al-Lubab*, 1:36-39) and al-Marghinani, *al-Hidaya*, 1:14-16 (= English trans. 1:14-19).

3. Vomiting a clot of blood.
4. Vomiting bile.

[4] **Body**:

1. Flowing blood.
2. Pus.
3. Serum.
4. Flesh.

- Other external cases where *wudu'* is invalidated include:

  1. **Sleep**: there are a few points to be made about sleeping and renewing the *wudu'*:[158]

"If one sleeps in a sitting posture with his buttocks firmly on the ground, his *wudu'* will not be invalidated. If he sleeps while sitting on a level platform but leaning upon a wall or a pillar (*ustuwana*), then Shams al-A'imma al-Halwani (Allah have mercy on him) stated that the most predominant position (*zahir al-madhhab*) of the School is that it does not invalidate the *wudu'*...."[159]

إذا نام قاعداً مسوياً إليتيه على الأرض لا ينتقض وضوءه، وإن نام قاعداً (على) مستوى الجلوس، ولكن مستنداً إلى جدار أو أسطوانة، ذكر شمس الأئمة الحلواني رحمه الله أن ظاهر المذهب أنه لا ينتقض وضوءه.

---

[158] For a detailed survey and analysis of the different juristic positions within the Hanafi school on this legal particular, see Alahazrat Imam Ahmed Reza Khan, *Nabah al-Qawm anna 'l-Wudu' min Ayyi Nawm*, pp.287-588.
[159] al-Bukhari, *al-Muhit al-Burhani*, 1, fol.7a.

- Sleeping while standing up does not invalidate *wudu'*.

- Sleeping while sitting does not invalidate *wudu'* if one is sitting on a hard surface where the buttocks are firmly pressed down (e.g. on a bench, floor, sofa, chair, settee, platform, etc.).

- Sleep while in prostration (*sajda*) does not invalidate *wudu'*.

- Swaying while sleeping does not invalidate the *wudu'*.

- Sleeping while lying on one's side or back or front invalidates *wudu'*.[160]

[Invalidation of *wudu'* continued...]

2. Fainting/losing consciousness (e.g. insanity, seizures, sedation, etc.).[161]

3. Intoxication (e.g. drunkenness, being stoned, etc.).[162]

4. Private parts rubbing together without a screen (but no penetration occurs).[163]

5. Audible/loud laughing such that another can hear.[164]

---

[160] See al-Marghinani, *al-Hidaya*, 1:15-16 (= English trans. 1:17-18) and al-Quduri, *al-Mukhtasar*, p.4 (= *al-Lubab*, 1:37-38).
[161] al-Shurunbulali, *Maraqi al-Falah*, p.37.
[162] al-Shurunbulali, *Maraqi al-Falah*, p.37.
[163] al-Shurunbulali, *Maraqi al-Falah*, p.38.
[164] al-Shurunbulali, *Nur al-Idah*, p.47.

§11. That which does not invalidate the *Wudu'*

- Blood that appears on the skin surface but does not flow.

- A peeled scab that does not bleed (e.g. blisters, pimples, etc.).

- If a worm exits a bodily wound or the ears or nose.

- Touching one's private parts.[165]

- Touching a woman.[166]

- Vomiting less than a mouthful.

- Vomiting phlegm or saliva even if it is a mouthful.

---

[165] See al-Bahlawi, *Adillat al-Hanafiyya.* pp.41-43 (#36-40 [with the citations of Imam al-Tahawi's chains of transmission); al-Sarakhsi, *Kitab al-Mabsut*, 1:66; Ibn al-Nujaym, *Bahr al-Ra'iq*, 1:45; Ibn al-Humam, *Fath al-Qadir* (= with its commentary), 1:45 and al-Kasani, *al-Bada'i` al-Sana'i*, 1:30.

[166] Bukhari, *Sahih* (#382) and Muslim, *Sahih* (#512) and al-Bahlawi, *Adillat al-Hanafiyya*, pp.40-41 (#33-35). Cf. the discussions by Ibn Hajar al-`Asqalani in *Talkhis al-Habir*, 3:136; al-Zayla`i, *Nasb al-Raya*, 1:73-74; al-Suyuti, *al-Jami` al-Saghir* (#7124) and al-Haythami, *Majma` al-Zawa'id*, 1:126.

§12. Miscellaneous injunctions of *Wudu'*

1. **Contact lenses**: these do not have to be removed because the eye ball is not considered part of the dimensions of the face required for washing.

2. **Nail polish**: this must be removed as it acts as a surface barrier because water must reach the required area to be washed.

3. **Hair gel**: this does not have to be washed out unless it is such that it prevents the hair from being wiped.

4. **Oils**: unless these solidify after a while, oil is not considered a barrier to the skin and hence does not need to be dried off.

5. **Hair dye**: this does not have to be removed or washed out in order to perform *wudu'* as the colour of the hair is not a factor pertaining to *wudu'*.

6. **Plaits, braids, extensions**: these do not have to be undone or removed in order to perform *wudu'* because the requirement is to wipe the head not to wash it.

7. **Paints, adhesives**: these will have to be removed as they are barriers to the surface of the skin and hence prevent water from contact.

SECTION 3: *GHUSL*
('FULL PURIFICATION BATH')

———— ◆ ————

- The primary text used as a basis for this section is the manual on Islamic Law as deduced by the Hanafi School entitled *Mukhtasar al-Quduri* ('The Abridged Book of Law') by the jurist and legal expert with the extensive interlinear commentary *al-Lubab fi Sharh al-Kitab* ('The Essence from the Commentary of the Book') by the eminent Shaykh `Abd al-Ghany al-Ghunaymi al-Maydani al-Nabulusi.

§1. Preliminaries and Definition of *Ghusl*

- One of the actions a believer performs as part of his ritual purification repertoire is *ghusl*.

- The meaning of *ghusl* is: 'washing the entire body thoroughly with water'.[167]

- There are many *hadith* texts regarding the mode or manner in which our beloved Prophet (Allah bless him and give him peace) performed the *ghusl*.

- One *hadith* reports it as follows:

From Ibn `Abbas from Maymuna bint al-Harith: "I placed water for the bath of the Prophet. He poured water on his left hand with his right and washed both. Then he washed his private parts.

صببت للنبي صلى الله عليه وسلم غسلا، فأفرغ بيمينه على يساره فغسلهما، ثم غسل فرجه، ثم قال بيده الأرض فمسحها

---

[167] Cf. al-Qal`aji, *Mu`jam Lughat al-Fuqaha'*, p.300.

Then he rubbed his hands over the earth and then washed it. He then rinsed his mouth and nose and then washed his face and poured water over his head. Then he stepped to the side and washed his feet...”[168]

بالتراب، ثم غسلها، ثم تمضمض واستنشق، ثم غسل وجهه، وأفاض على رأسه، ثم تنحى، فغسل قدميه، ثم أتي بمنديل، فلم ينفض بها...

- From the *hadith* text above, we have the following actions of the Prophet:

1) Beginning from the right.

2) Washing the hands.

3) Washing the private parts.

4) Rinsing the mouth and nose.

5) Washing the face.

6) Washing the feet.

---

[168] Bukhari, *Sahih* (#259).

§2. That which obligates the *Ghusl*

- Allah states in the Qur'an al-Karim 5:6:

يَا أَيُّهَا الَّذِينَ آمَنُوا إِذَا قُمْتُمْ إِلَى الصَّلَاةِ فَاغْسِلُوا وُجُوهَكُمْ وَأَيْدِيَكُمْ إِلَى

الْمَرَافِقِ وَامْسَحُوا بِرُءُوسِكُمْ وَأَرْجُلَكُمْ إِلَى الْكَعْبَيْنِ وَإِنْ كُنْتُمْ جُنُبًا فَاطَّهَّرُوا ۝

*{O you who believe! when you rise up to perform the prayer, wash your faces and wash your hands as far as the elbows and wipe your heads and wash your feet to the ankles. **And if you are in a state of ritual impurity, then purify yourself completely**...}*

- Imam al-Quduri in his *al-Mukhtasar* states what obligates *ghusl*:

"The incidents which obligate *ghusl* are: [1] Emission of semen accompanied by spurting and excitement from a man or a woman. [2] Contact of the two circumcised parts (*iltiqa' al-khitanayn bi-ghayri inzal*) even without any ejaculation. [3] Menstruation and [4] Post-birth bleeding (*al-nifas*)."[169]

والمعاني الموجبة الغسل إنزال المني على وجه الدفق والشهوة من الرجل والمرأة والتقاء الختانين من غير إنزال والحيض والنفاس.

---

[169] al-Quduri, *Mukhtasar*, p.5 (= *al-Lubab* of al-Maydani, 1:39-42); al-Marghinani, *al-Hidaya*, 1:16-19 (= English trans. 1:19-23); See Z. Mahmood, *The Book of Taharah*, pp.38-44, F. F. Rabbani, *The Absolute Essentials of Islam*, pp.11-13 and M. I. Attar, *The Laws of Salah*, Rasail-e-Attaria, 1:51-69.

- The major ritual bath then is obligatory (*fard*) when one of the following eight occurs:[170]

  1. Full emission of sperm (*mani*) such that it is caused by arousal and self-stimulation.[171]

  2. Sexual intercourse.

  3. The frontal area of the penis disappears into the vagina or anus.

  4. If one awakes from sleep knowing he was not erect prior to sleeping and was not sure he had a dream and sees wetness/thin liquid.

  5. If one believes he has discharged sperm having concluded that after regaining consciousness or sobering up.

  6. When a female's menstrual period ends.

  7. When a female concludes her post-natal bleeding.

  8. Death (i.e. the body has to be washed).

---

[170] See al-Shurunbulali, *Nur al-Idah*, p.54 and idem, *Maraqi al-Sa`adat*, p.49.

[171] Ibn `Abidin, *Radd al-Muhtar*, 1:159:

"His statement: (**and the semen of men is white...**) and their semen is also thick whereas the semen of women is thinner."

قوله (ومنيه أبيض الخ) وأيضا منيه خاثر ومنيها رقيق...

§3. That which does not obligate the *Ghusl*

- *Madhi* (prostatic fluid/pre-coital fluid which is not semen).[172]

- *Wadi* (white cloudy fluid before urine emission or after sexual intercourse).[173]

- If one has a sexual dream but finds no wetness (nocturnal emissions).

- Giving birth without visible bleeding.

---

[172] al-Shurunbulali, *Nur al-Idah*, pp.55-56. In the *Radd al-Muhtar*, 1:335 of Imam Ibn 'Abidin, it states:

"Regarding his statement [s: i.e. that of Imam al-Haskafi]: (**and not in the case of *madhi***) meaning it is not obligatory to perform the *ghusl* if *madhi* is emitted [...] which is said to be a thin clear liquid that is released at the point of excitement not by it and in women it is stronger and given the name *qadhi*..."	(قوله : لا عند مذي) أي لا يفرض الغسل عند خروج مذي كظبي بمعجمة ساكنة وياء مخففة على الأفصح، وفيه الكسر مع التخفيف والتشديد، وقيل هما لحن ماء رقيق أبيض يخرج عند الشهوة لا بها، وهو في النساء أغلب، قيل هو منهن يسمى القذى بمفتوحتين نهر.

[173] Ibn 'Abidin mentions a description of *wady* in *Radd al-Muhtar*, 1:165

"He mentioned four responses the last one being that *wady* is that sticky fluid exits after one has a bath due to having sexual intercourse or after urinating as explained in *al-Khazana* and *al-Tabyin* [...]."	وذكر أربعة أجوبة أخر منها أن الودي ما يخرج بعد الاغتسال من الجماع وبعد البول وهو شيء لزج كذا فسره في الخزانة والتبيين فالإشكال إنما يرد على من اقتصر في تفسيره على ما يخرج بعد البول...

- Insertion of the penis into the vagina but with a barrier that prevents the sensation of pleasure.

- If a man neither penetrates a virgin girl nor orgasms or impairs her hymen.

- Administering medicine into the vagina anus.

- Swearing, lying, cheating, etc.

- Improper behaviour.

§4. The Obligatory aspects of *Ghusl*

- Shaykh Zadah in *Majma` al-Anhur* lists the types of *ghusl* and their rulings:

"Know that the *ghusl* is performed in 11 cases: 4 cases being *fard* which include: [1] Performing a bath after penetration – front or rear [...] [2] Performing a bath after ejaculation caused by any means of excitement and gratification [...] [3] Performing a bath due to Menstruation. [4] Performing a bath due to post-natal bleeding. 4 cases being *sunna* such as: [5] Performing a bath on Friday, [6] the two Eid days, [7] while in a state of *ihram* whether for Hajj or `Umra and [8] the day of `Arafa. 2 cases when it is *wajib*: [9] when washing the dead and [10] when washing impurities [...] and an instance where it is considered *mustahabb* and they number many [...]".[174]

وَاعْلَمْ أَنَّ الْغُسْلَ عَلَى أَحَدَ عَشَرَ وَجْهًا أَرْبَعَةٌ فَرِيضَةٌ وَهُوَ الْغُسْلُ مِنَ الْإِيلَاجِ فِي قُبُلٍ أَوْ دُبُرٍ إِذَا غَابَتِ الْحَشَفَةُ عَلَى الْفَاعِلِ وَالْمَفْعُولِ بِهِ أَنْزَلَ أَوْ لَمْ يُنْزِلْ وَالثَّانِي الْغُسْلُ مِنَ الْإِنْزَالِ عَنْ شَهْوَةٍ بِأَيِّ وَجْهٍ كَانَ مِنْ إِتْيَانِ بَهِيمَةٍ أَوْ مُعَالَجَةِ الذَّكَرِ بِالْيَدِ أَوْ بِالِاحْتِلَامِ أَوْ بِالْقُبْلَةِ أَوْ بِاللَّمْسِ لِشَهْوَةٍ ، وَالرَّجُلُ وَالْمَرْأَةُ فِي ذَلِكَ سَوَاءٌ وَالثَّالِثُ الْغُسْلُ مِنَ الْحَيْضِ وَالرَّابِعُ الْغُسْلُ مِنَ النَّفَاسِ وَأَرْبَعَةٌ مِنْهُ سُنَّةٌ غُسْلُ الْجُمُعَةِ وَغُسْلُ الْعِيدَيْنِ وَغُسْلُ الْإِحْرَامِ سَوَاءٌ كَانَ إِحْرَامَ حَجَّةٍ أَوْ عُمْرَةٍ وَغُسْلُ يَوْمِ عَرَفَةَ لِلْوُقُوفِ وَغُسْلَانِ وَاجِبَانِ غُسْلُ الْمَوْتَى وَغُسْلُ النَّجَاسَةِ إِذَا كَانَتْ أَكْثَرَ مِنْ قَدْرِ الدِّرْهَمِ فِي الْمُغَلَّظَةِ وَرُبُعِ الثَّوْبِ فِي الْمُخَفَّفَةِ وَغُسْلٌ مُسْتَحَبٌّ وَهُوَ كَثِيرٌ مِنْ

---

[174] Shaykh Zadah, *Majma` al-Anhur*, 1:28-30.

ذَلِكَ غُسْلُ الْكَافِرِ وَالْكَافِرَةِ إِذَا أَسْلَمَا

وَالصَّبِيُّ وَالصَّبِيَّةِ إِذَا أَدْرَكَا بِالسِّنِّ وَكَذَا

الْمَجْنُونُ إِذَا أَفَاقَ.

- The full ritual of *ghusl*, involves three basic obligatory aspects (*fara'id*) and they are:[175]

Obligatory Aspects of *Ghusl*

[1]	[2]	[3]
Madmada	*Istinshaq*	*Isalat al-ma' `ala 'l-zahir al-badn*
Rinsing the mouth	Sniffing water up the nostrils and then spraying it out.	Pouring water over the entire outer body.

- *Madmada* / المضمضة : this involves rinsing the entire mouth as mentioned in the *fiqh* manuals:

"One of the obligatory aspects of *ghusl* is washing the entire mouth".[176]

فرض الغسل غسل كل فمه...

"The technical definition of *madmada* is to rinse water around the entire mouth."[177]

المضمضة اصطلاحا استيعاب الماء جميع الفم...

---

[175] Taken from Alahazrat Imam Ahmed Reza Khan's *Khulasat Tibyan al-Wudu'*, pp.593-599.
[176] al-Haskafi, *Durr al-Mukhtar*, 1:28.
[177] Ibn `Abidin, *Radd al-Muhtar*, 1:78.

- *Istinshaq* / الإستنشاق : this involves pulling water up to the nostrils and then to spray it out of the nose:

"The technical definition of *istinshaq* is enabling water to reach the two soft openings of the nose [s: i.e. the nostrils; *marin*] [...]."[178]

الإستنشاق اصطلاحا ايصال الماء الى المارن...

"The 'marin' is defined as being the two soft openings of the nose..."[179]

المارن ما لان من الانف...

- *Isalat al-ma' `ala 'l-zahir al-badn* / إسالة الماء على ظاهر البدن : this involves the entire external body parts to be washed or to have water poured over it:

"[...] washing means to pour water over the body so that there is dripping."[180]

غسل اي اسالة الماء مع التقاطر...

Water reaching the entire body means that water must reach the following areas:

1.	2.	3.	4.
The inner area of the penis, i.e. the circumcised part. The outer part	Any cavity in the body, e.g. armpits, inner area of the naval, etc.	For men, any braids or plaits must be untied so water can reach	Water must reach underneath the beard, moustache and eyebrows.

---

[178] Ibn `Abidin, *Radd al-Muhtar*, 1:78-79.
[179] Ibn `Abidin, *Radd al-Muhtar*, 1:79.
[180] al-Haskafi, *Durr al-Mukhtar*, 1:28.

of the vagina must be washed (although the inner is not necessary). roots although women do not have to untie their braids and plaits provided the water does reach the roots.

- To rub water into the skin is not sufficient to constitute 'washing'.[181]

- To use water such that no water drips from the body is not sufficient to constitute 'washing'.[182]

---

[181] Ibn `Abidin, *Radd al-Muhtar*, 1:65.
[182] Ibn `Abidin, *Radd al-Muhtar*, 1:65.

§5. The *Sunna* aspects of *Ghusl*

- The *sunna* procedure or actions of the Messenger of Allah in *ghusl* are the following:

"The *sunna* actions of *ghusl* are that the one performing *ghusl*: [1] Begin with washing his hands and genitals. [2] Remove filth if it is on his body, then [3] Perform *wudu'* like the *wudu'* for *salah*, except for his feet, then [4] Pour water over the rest of his body three times, then [5] Step aside from that place and then wash his feet".[183]

وسنة الغسل : أن يبتدئ المغتسل فيغسل يديه وفرجه ويزيل نجاسة إن كانت على بدنه ثم يتوضأ وضوءه للصلاة إلا رجليه ثم يفيض الماء على رأسه وسائر جسده ثلاثا ثم يتنحى عن ذلك المكان فيغسل رجليه.

- Therefore, the blessed *Sunna* aspects of *ghusl* are:

1. To make intention.

2. To begin by washing the hands and private parts.[184]

3. Removing filth from the body.[185]

4. Performing *wudu'* like that for the *salah* for the *ghusl*.[186]

5. Pouring water over the body three times from the right shoulder and rubbing the body.[187]

---

[183] al-Quduri, *Mukhtasar*, p.5 (= *al-Lubab* of al-Maydani, 1:39-42).

[184] Tirmidhi, *Sunan* (#41).

[185] al-Haythami, *Majma` al-Zawa'id*, 1:275.

[186] Muslim, *Sahih* (#474).

[187] Bukhari, *Sahih* (#251).

6. Stepping aside to wash the feet.[188]

- There are times when performing *ghusl* is considered *sunna*, they include:

- al-Quduri states in *al-Mukhtasar*:

"The Messenger of Allah (Allah bless him and grant him peace) made *ghusl sunna* for: [1] the Jumu'a day. [2] The Two Eids and [3] *Ihram*."[189]	وسن رسول الله صلى الله عليه وسلم الغسل للجمعة والعيدين والإحرام.

- There are also other times when it is recommended/desirable (*mustahabb/mandub*) to perform *ghusl*:[190]

1) When someone embraces Islam and h/she is free from major ritual impurity.

2) When one attains maturity of age.

3) When one recovers from any form of insanity, intoxication or unconsciousness.

4) After one has been in a cupping session (*hijama*).

5) After washing a dead body.

6) On the Night of *Nisf min Sha'ban* (['Middle Night of Sha'ban' = *laylat al-bara'a*]).

---

[188] Bukhari, *Sahih* (#272).
[189] al-Quduri, *Mukhtasar*, p.6 (= *al-Lubab* of al-Maydani, 1:40-42) and al-Marghinani, *al-Hidaya*, 1:17-19 (= English trans. 1:19-23).
[190] See al-Shurunbulali, *Nur al-Idah*, p.60-62.

7) The Night of al-Qadr.

8) Upon entering Medina – the City of the Master of the two worlds the Holy Prophet.

9) The 10th Dhu 'l-Hijja morning at Muzdalifa.

10) When entering Makkah for *tawaf al-ziyara* (or any *tawaf* in general).

11) The Prayer for the solar eclipse (*salat al-kusuf al-shams*) and lunar eclipse (*salat al-kusuf al-qamr*).

12) When seeking rain (*salat al-istisqa'*).

13) When there is fear, strong winds or overwhelming darkness in the day.

14) Upon returning from a journey.

15) The *mawlid* occasion ('The Prophet's birthday').

16) For any blessed gathering.

17) For wearing new clothes.

§6. The *adab* aspects of *Ghusl*

- The *adab* of *ghusl* (and the disliked aspects [*makruhat*]) are the same as in *wudu'* [refer to Section 2 on *wudu'* above] with the exception that one does not face the *qibla* ('direction of the Holy Ka`ba') in *ghusl* because in most cases a person will be naked when performing *ghusl*.[191]

- Some additional rules pertaining to *ghusl* include:

  1) *Ghusl* should be made in a place of total privacy.

  2) *Ghusl* may be performed standing or seated, preferably seated.

  3) Use sufficient water. Do not skimp nor be wasteful.

  4) Abstain from speaking whilst performing *ghusl*.

  5) It is better not to read any *kalmia, du`as* ('supplication') or *ayah* ('verses of the Qur'an') while bathing.

  6) Before performing *ghusl* one should make *niyya* ('intention') thus: 'I am performing *ghusl* to become ritually pure.'

  7) Without *niyya* there is no *thawab* ('reward') although *ghusl* will be valid.

  8) All parts of the body should be rubbed with the hands to ensure that water has reached all parts of the body and no portion is left dry.

---

[191] See al-Shurunbulali, *Nur al-Idah*, pp.59-60.

9) Rings, earrings, etc. should be removed to ensure that no portion covered by them is left dry. The navel and ears must all be wet. If they are not wet *ghusl* will be incomplete.

10) On completion one should confine oneself to a clean place. If, while performing *wudu'* the feet had been washed, it is not necessary to wash them again. Dry the body with a clean towel and dress as hastily as possible.

11) If after *ghusl* one recalls that a certain portion of the body is left dry. It is not necessary to repeat the *ghusl*. Merely washing the dry portion is sufficient. It is not sufficient, however, to pass a wet hand over the dry place. If one has forgotten to rinse the mouth or the nostrils, these too must be rinsed when recalled after *ghusl* has been performed.[192]

---

[192] From *Talim al-Haq*, pp.35-36 (with minor changes) and Alahazrat Imam Ahmed Reza Khan, *Khulasat Tibyan al-Wudu'*, pp.602-604.

§7. The *Makruhat* of *Ghusl*

1. Facing the *qibla*.

2. To make *ghusl* in a place where non-Muslims can see.

3. To talk while performing the *ghusl*.

4. Wasting water or using very little water.

5. Splashing water on one's body.

6. Getting help without a need.

§8. Miscellaneous injunctions of *Ghusl*

1. **Braids and plaits**: men have to undo their plaits in order to allow water to reach the roots and the entire hair surfaces in between the hair but women do not have to; water only has to reach the roots for them.[193]

2. **Fillings and braces**: if the filings and braces are non-removable then *ghusl* will be permitted with them based on the principle of necessity (*darura*).[194]

3. **Showers**: the ruling of taking a shower takes the ruling of flowing water. If one stands under a shower for the duration it takes to perform *wudu'*, then the *ghusl* will be valid provided the mouth and nose is also rinsed.[195]

4. **Soaps and shampoos**: any cleaning product such as body washes, soaps, shampoos and oils may be used when performing *ghusl* provided the ingredients are lawful.

5. **Bandages and wounds**: If by unwrapping the bandage(s) it will seriously harm and affect the wound, then it is sufficient to merely wipe over the area of it. Whenever possible, one should remove any coverings (bandages, patches, plasters, splinters, etc) **UNLESS** it is harmful and extremely difficult.[196]

---

[193] See al-Shurunbulali, *Maraqi al-Falah*, p.138 and passim.
[194] See Ahmad Reza Khan, *al-Fatawa al-Ridwiyya*, 2:453.
[195] See Ibn `Abidin, *Radd al-Muhtar*, 1:320.
[196] See al-Tahtawi's marginalia on the *Maraqi al-Falah*, p.143.

SECTION 4: *TAYAMMUM* ('DRY ABLUTION')

———— ♦ ————

- The primary text used as a basis for this section is the primer on Hanafi devotional injunctions entitled *Nur al-Idah* ('The Light of Clarification') by the Qadi of Egypt Imam al-Shurunbulali with his own interlinear commentary of the manual entitled *Maraqi al-Falah* ('The Ascent to Felicity').

§1. Definitions and Preliminaries

- Linguistically, the word 'tayammum' means 'absolute intention' (*al-qasdu mutlaqan*). Thus, the phrase: *yammama shatra al-masjid* – 'he set out to the Mosque' – means *qasadahu* ('he intended to go to it'). So, in *sura* al-Baqara:267 Allah (swt) says: {*And do not **aim** to spend from the bad things...*} meaning 'do not intend (*la taqsudu*) to spend from the bad things (*mal al-radi*').'[197]

- The shari'a definition of 'tayammum' is: "wiping the face and hands with pure earth in a specified manner" (*mash al-wajh wa 'l-yadayn bi-turab tuhur 'ala wajh makhsus*).[198]

---

[197] See al-Shawkani, *Fath al-Qadir: al-Jami' bayn al-Fanni al-Riwaya wa 'l-Diraya fi 'Ilm al-Tafsir*, p.247; al-Nasafi, *Madarik al-Tanzil wa Haqa'iq al-Ta'wil*, p.138; al-Baydawi, *Anwar al-Tanzil wa Asrar al-Ta'wil*, 1:140; al-'Izz al-Din 'Abd al-'Aziz b.'Abd al-Salam in his *Tafsir al-Qur'an*, p.72; al-Zamakhshari, *al-Kashshaf 'an Haqa'iq al-Tanzil wa 'Uyun al-Aqawil fi Wujuh al-Ta'wil*, 2:10-11 and al-Baghawi, *Ma'alim al-Tanzil*, 1:255.

[198] See 'Abd al-Rahman al-Jaziri, *Kitab al-Fiqh 'ala Madhahib al-Arba'a*, 1:148. The Malikis and the Shafi'is add the act of intention (*niyya*) because they consider it to be one of the pillars of *tayammum* (*rukn min arkan*).

- *Tayammum* has been especially bestowed upon this *umma* both as a 'strict ordinance' (`*azima*) and as an 'exemption' (*rukhsa*).

- Some scholars have commented that it is the former only in the absence of water (*li-`adam al-ma'*) and the latter when one has a valid excuse (*li 'l-`uzr*).[199]

- The Qur'an al-Karim mentions *tayammum* in 5:6:

وَإِنْ كُنْتُمْ مَرْضَىٰ أَوْ عَلَىٰ سَفَرٍ أَوْ جَاءَ أَحَدٌ مِنْكُمْ مِنَ الْغَائِطِ أَوْ لَامَسْتُمُ النِّسَاءَ فَلَمْ تَجِدُوا مَاءً فَتَيَمَّمُوا صَعِيدًا طَيِّبًا فَامْسَحُوا بِوُجُوهِكُمْ وَأَيْدِيكُمْ مِنْهُ ۚ مَا يُرِيدُ اللَّهُ لِيَجْعَلَ عَلَيْكُمْ مِنْ حَرَجٍ وَلَٰكِنْ يُرِيدُ لِيُطَهِّرَكُمْ وَلِيُتِمَّ نِعْمَتَهُ عَلَيْكُمْ لَعَلَّكُمْ تَشْكُرُونَ

{...*And if [any of] you are ill, travelling or come after performing the call of nature or [if] you have been in contact with women or do not find water,* **then perform the dry ablution with pure earth, wiping your faces, arms with it**...}

- In the noble *hadith*, the Prophet (SAW) states:

| From Umama (Allah be well pleased with him) that the Prophet (Allah bless him and grant him peace) said: "**The whole earth was made a Pure[200] Mosque[201] for me** | [...] و جعلت [لي] الأرض مساجد وطهورا أينما أدركتني الصلاة تمسحت وصليت... |

---

[199] al-Shawkani, *Nayl al-Awtar: Sharh Muntaqa al-Akhbar min Ahahdith al-Sayyid al-Akhyar*, 1:191.

[200] The property 'tuhuran' (طهورا) means 'pure', 'clean' and 'unadulterated.' Hence, from this statement, the Hanafi scholars deduce the ruling that earth can eliminate impurity (*al-turab yarfa`u 'l-hadath*) just like water. Hence, for them, unlike the other scholars of the *madhabs*, *tayammum* eliminates impurity like *wudu'* and *ghusl* and one

**and my *umma*. When a
person from my *umma*
desires to perform the
Prayer, he has for him a
mosque and something
pure."**[202]

- The permissibility of performing *tayammum* from
  any part of the earth is thus allowed from the above
  text because the word 'al-ard' ('earth') is general
  ('*umum*) in its purport i.e. 'all of it' (*li-jami'iha*).[203]

- The grammatical corroboration (*al-tawkid al-
  ma'nawi*) 'kulluha' – 'all of it' – is said to add
  emphasis (*ta'kid*) to the permissibility, thus the
  statement in the *hadith* could be re-written as: 'the
  earth was made pure for me - <u>all of it</u>.'

---

may therefore make the intention of seeking purification when
performing the *tayammum*.

[201] The term 'masjidan' (مسجدا/mosque) here is said to mean either the
'place of prostration' (*mawdu' sujud*) without specification as to where
(i.e. not necessarily in a mosque) or a metaphorical (*majazan*)
interpretation which is that the Prayer, once it is permitted in its entirety,
becomes like a mosque in itself, i.e. a 'self-contained, fixed and
established place of worship' (*makan al-mubniy li 'l-salah*).

[202] Narrated by Ahmad in his *Musnad*, 2/222 and 5/248. See also al-
Shawkani, *Nayl al-Awtar*, 1:193; Abu Dawud, *Sunan* (#489); Tirmidhi,
Sunan (#318) and Ibn Majah, *Sunan* (#745). As a point in passing, the
verb in the *hadith* is in the passive form (*ju'ila*) which may mean that this
favour Allah bestowed upon the Prophet's *umma* was already ordained
and hence precludes any abrogation. The entire earth will always remain
pure and a place to pray for the Muslims. The last two *hadiths*, Tirmidhi
(#318) and Ibn Majah (#745) do add the qualification (but not
abrogation): "except the graves and the bathrooms" (*illa 'l-maqbara wa
'l-hammam*). Cf. also Bukhari, *Sahih* (#335, 438 & 3122) and finally al-
Nawawi, *Sharh Sahih Musim*, p.497.

[203] The definite article ال (the *alif* is merely prosthetic) is said here to
denote generally *al-ta'rif* ('definition') but more specifically it denotes
'familiarity' (*li 'l-'ahd*), so the meaning would be *this* earth that we
inhabit is entirely pure.

- Moreover, the narration above from the *Musnad* (2/222) has the verb 'tamassahtu' (تمسحت) meaning 'I wipe my self' and 'sallaytu' (صليت) meaning 'I pray' hence the Prophet (SAW) used the earth as a source for purifying himself to perform an act of obligation.[204]

- The Prophet stated:

`Abd Allah b. Yusuf narrated to us who said: Malik b. `Abd al-Rahman b. al-Qasim reported to us from his father from `A'isha (ra) the wife of the Prophet (SAW) [who] said:	خرجنا مع رسول الله صلى الله عليه وسلم في بعض أسفاره، حتى إذا كنا بالبيداء، أو بذات الجيش، انقطع عقد لي ، فأقام رسول الله صلى الله عليه وسلم على
We went out with the Prophet on one of his journeys until we were in [a place called] al-Bayda' whereupon one of my bracelets broke, so the Prophet began looking for it and some of the people began to look for it with him. There was also no water. The people then went to Abu Bakr al-Siddiq and complained: 'Have you seen what `A'isha has done?' She began looking with the Prophet and the people [for water] but there was not any water nor did they have any with them.' So, Abu Bakr	التماسه ، وأقام الناس معه، وليسوا على ماء، وليس معهم ماء، فأتى الناس إلى أبي بكر الصديق فقالوا : ألا ترى ما صنعت عائشة ، أقامت برسول الله صلى الله عليه وسلم وبالناس، وليسوا على ماء، وليس معهم ماء؟ فجاء أبو بكر، ورسول الله صلى الله عليه وسلم واضع رأسه على فخذي قد نام، فقال : حبست رسول الله

---

[204] For a fuller commentary, see al-Shawkani, *Nayl al-Awtar*, 1:193-294.

came to me while the Prophet was asleep resting his head on my thigh. [Abu Bakr] said: 'you prevented the Messenger of Allah and the people while there neither was any water nor had they any with them.' `A'isha said: 'Abu Bakr blamed me and said whatever Allah willed him to say and he also poked me in the side with his hand. He did not prevent me from moving except that the Prophet was [resting his head] upon my thigh. <u>The Prophet got up when it was the morning without water and then Allah revealed the verse of *tayammum* and so we performed the *tayammum*.</u>

Usayd b. Hudayr said that: 'it was not the first blessing for the family of Abu Bakr.' `A'isha said: 'the camel I was on, got up and we found the necklace underneath it'."[205]

صلى الله عليه وسلم والناس، وليسوا على ماء وليس معهم ماء . قالت عائشة : فعاتبني أبو بكر، وقال ما شاء الله أن يقول، وجعل يطعنني بيده في خاصرتي، ولا يمنعني من التحرك إلا مكان رسول الله صلى الله عليه وسلم على فخذي، فقام رسول الله صلى الله عليه وسلم حين أصبح على غير ماء، فأنزل الله آية التيمم، فقال أسيد بن حضير : ما هي بأول بركتكم يا آل أبي بكر . قالت : فبعثنا البعير الذي كنت عليه فإذا العقد تحته.

---

[205] Bukhari, *Sahih* (#334).

§2. The conditions of *Tayammum*

- The ritual act of *Tayammum* is valid with 8 conditions (*shurut*). They are the following:[206]

"There are eight conditions for the validity of *tayammum* and they are: [1] Intention... [2] One who has a legitimate excuse to perform *tayammum*... [3] It should be performed with a pure earthly substance... [4] That all the required area be covered... [5] One should perform the wiping with the entire hand or the greater part of it ... [6] To gently strike one's palms on the earth twice ... [7] The termination of those things which are incompatible with *tayammum* ... [8] The removal of those things which prevent wiping...."[207]

باب التيمم شروط صحته يصح التيمم بشروط ثمانية الأول النية ...الثاني العذر المبيح للتيمم ... الثالث أن يكون التيمم بطاهر من جنس الأرض... الربع استيعاب المحل بالمسح... الخامس أن يمسح بجميع اليد... السادس أن يكون بضربتين بباطن الكفين... السابع انقطاع ما ينافيه... الثامن زوال ما يمنع المسح...

---

[206] For references, see al-Quduri, *al-Mukhtasar*, pp.12-15 (= *al-Lubab*, 1:5); al-Marghinani, *al-Hidaya*, 1:26-29 (= English trans. 1:43-51); al-Mawsili, *Ta`lil al-Mukhtar*, 1: 27-29 and Alahazrat Imam Ahmad Reza Khan, *Husn al-Ta`mmum li-Bayan Hadd al-Tayammum*, pp.311-410 for an extremely elaborate assessment of the integrals pertaining to *tayammum*.

[207] al-Shurunbulali, *Nur al-Idah*, pp.63-66 and idem, *Maraqi al-Sa`adat*, pp.50-52.See also al-Mawsili's *al-Ikhtiyar*, 1:20:

(مَنْ لَمْ يَقْدِرْ عَلَى اسْتِعْمَالِ الْمَاءِ لِبُعْدِهِ مِيلًا أَوْ لِمَرَضٍ أَوْ بَرْدٍ أَوْ خَوْفِ عَدُوٍّ أَوْ عَطَشٍ أَوْ عَدَمِ آلَةٍ يَسْتَقِي بِهَا، (يَتَيَمَّمُ بِمَا كَانَ مِنْ أَجْزَاءِ الْأَرْضِ كَالتُّرَابِ وَالرَّمْلِ وَالْجِصِّ وَالْكُحْلِ)

1. The intention (al-niyya):[208]

"[The intention] commences the moment one strikes that with which one will perform the *tayammum*. The valid conditions of the intention are three: 1] that one is a Muslim (*al-islam*); 2] the discernment [of the words one is uttering] and 3] knowledge of what is being intended (*al-`ilm bi-ma yanwih*). Moreover, one of three things is a condition for the validity of *tayammum* in order to perform the Prayer. 1] the intention to be purified (*niyyat al-tahara*); 2] to be legally fit for the Prayer (*istibahah li 'l-salah*) and 3] the intention of a specific act of worship (*niyyat `ibadatin maqsudin*) that would otherwise not be valid without purification; thus one is not permitted to pray if one makes the intention for *tayammum* only or makes the intention to only read the Qur'an[209] while not being in a state of major ritual impurity."[210]

وشروط صحة النية ثلاثة الإسلام والتمييز

والعلم بما ينويه ويشترط لصحة نية التيمم

للصلاة به أحد ثلاثة أشياء إما نية الطهارة

أو استباحة الصلاة أو نية عبادة مقصودة

لا تصح بدون طهارة فلا يصلى به إذا

نوى التيمم فقط أو نواه لقراءة القرآن ولم

يكن جنبا...

---

[208] Imam al-Quduri states that the intention for *taymmum* is obligatory (*fard*), *al-Lubab*, 1:53. This is because one is seeking to be purified with materials that are not pure (*mulawwath*) or are not pure of itself (*bi-nafsihi*) whereas water is created pure which is why no intention according to the Hanafis is required for *wudu'*. al-Shurunbulali, *Maraqi al-Falah*, p.47.

[209] Mere recitation of the Qur'an does not necessitate legal purity.

[210] al-Shurunbulali, *Maraqi al-Falah*, pp.47-48.

2. Fulfilling the status of exemption:

    a. A person being approximately a mile (*mil*)[211] from where water can be found.[212]

    b. Fear of becoming ill (*husul al-marad*).[213]

---

[211] al-Quduri, *Mukhtasar*, pp.13-14 (= *al-Lubab*, 1:51) and al-Shurunbulali, *Maraqi al-Falah*, p.48. A 'mil' ('mile') amounts to about 4000 milestones; in other words, a distance such that it would be a hardship or not feasible to acquire the water. Some argue it is a distance of a half hour walk. See Tahtawi on the margins of *Maraqi al-Falah*, 1:169.

[212] The verse of *surat* al-Ma'ida explicitly permits this. The legality (*mashru`iyya*) of *tayammum* for the Prayer when water is not found is established in Bukhari, *Sahih* (#348 & 3571). See also al-Nawawi, *al-Minhaj*, p.590. The explicit wording (`ibarat al-nass*) of the text indicates the permissibility of one who is in a major ritual impurity (*junub*) i.e. in need of *ghusl* to perform the *tayammum*. Although not explicitly stated, a necessary inference of the text is that one who is only in need of *wudu'* can also perform *tayammum* in the absence of water because if the state of greater impurity is given concession so too must the state of lesser impurity. This inference is known as *isharat al-nass* ('alluded meaning') according to the Hanafi jurists and *qiyas al-awla* ('greater analogy') amongst the Shafi`i jurists. See Imam al-Qadi Nizam al-Din al-Shashi, *Usul al-Shashi*, pp.80-81. Another *hadith* also indicates the permissibility of *tayammum* particularly if one incurs a wound (*jarh*); see Abu Dawud, *Sunan* (#336); the *Sunan* of al-Daraqutni 1:190 as well as al-Shawkani's *Nayl al-Awtar*, 1:191.

[213] That is, one who can find water but fears that if he uses the water, it will intensify his illness (*ishtidad al-marad*). Any person who is in a state of major ritual impurity (*junub*) is also exempted if he fears that the water from a full bath will kill him. See Abu Dawud, *Sunan* (#334) where `Amr b. al-`As (ra) after a wet dream did not perform *ghusl* for fear that the extreme cold might kill him so he performed *tayammum* and prayed with the other companions. When he narrated the incident to the Prophet (Allah bless him and grant him peace), the Prophet simply laughed and said nothing. The strongest *qarina* ('contextual indication') for a silent approval by the Prophet is 'laughter' (*al-tabassum*) and 'rejoicing' (*al-istibshar*). Moreover, Sufyan al-Thawri, Imam Abu Hanifa and Malik have deduced the permissibility of not repeating the Prayer as the Prophet did not command `Amr b. al-`As to do so because if the repetition of the Prayer was obligatory, then the Prophet would have been obliged to disclose it. There are no other concomitant narrations for the obligation

c. When a person fears there may be an enemy (`aduw`) around the vicinity.[214]

d. When there is a possibility of suffering from extreme thirst (`atsh`).[215]

e. When there is a possibility of suffering from extreme coldness.[216]

f. Wounds on most of the body.

g. When fearing that the time for the `Id Prayer may expire if one preoccupies himself with wudu' (law ishtaghala bi 'l-wudu').

h. When the Funeral Prayer (janaza) will elude a person.[217]

i. When one fears there will be insufficient water for say cooking or making meals.

j. Loss of equipments or tools (li-faqd alah) such as a rope to get water out of the well or any other means that prevents a person from using or obtaining water with relative ease.

---

of repeating the Prayer; see al-Shawkani, *Nayl al-Awtar*, 1:193. Bukhari has the same narration but in *mu`allaq* ('shorter') form, p.60.

[214] Ibn `Abidin, *Radd al-Muhtar*, 1:157.

[215] Ibn `Abidin, *Radd al-Muhtar*, 1:156

[216] Ibn `Abidin, *Radd al-Muhtar*, 1:157.

[217] However, one **may not** perform *tayammum* if one fears the Friday Prayer will elude him or the time will lapse. He simply performs *wudu'* and attempts to catch the Prayer. If he misses it, then he must pray the four *rak`at* ('units') of the *Zuhr* Prayer. See Ibn `Abidin, *Radd al-Muhtar*, 1:157. See also Abu Dawud, *Sunan* (#334-335); Ahmad in his *Musnad*, 4/203; al-Daraqutni, *Sunan*, 1:178 as well as al-Shawkani, *Nayl al-Awtar*, 1:192.

3. Pure earth substance must be used (*bi-zahirin min jins al-ard*):[218] The types of earth include:

   a. Dry earth (*turab*),
   b. Stones (*hajar*),
   c. Sand (*raml*)
   d. Limestone (*jissa/kilis*).[219]
   e. Clay pots.
   f. Marble.
   g. Baked earthen pots (even if washed and they have no dust).
   h. Walls of mud, stone or brick.
   i. Any item which has thick dust on it.

- Materials such as wood (*khatab*), silver (*fidda*), gold (*dhahab*), iron (*hadid*) as well as copper (*nahhas*) are not permitted for *tayammum*.[220]

- Also, the following item too cannot be used for *tayammum*:

   j. Glass.
   k. Food items.
   l. Anything item that rots.
   m. Any item that melts.

---

[218] This is the opinion of Imam Abu Hanifa and Imam Hasan al-Shaybani.

[219] Imam Abu Yusuf, however, only permits the use of sand and dry earth. al-Ghunaymi, *al-Lubab*, 1:53 and al-Shurunbulali, *Maraqi al-Falah*, p.49.

[220] The rule is that any material that is combustible is not permitted because the verse states *sa'idan tayyiban* (al-Nisa':43). The word 'sa'idan' is interpreted by the majority of the scholars to be the 'surface of the earth' and 'tayyiban' to mean 'natural, good and wholesome'. Cf. *surat* al-Kahf:40 where Allah says *sa'idan zalaqan* – 'a slippery surface [or rock]' (*hajar amlas*). The Hanbali scholars only permit the use of dry earth but allow, for reasons of necessity, the other elements. See Ibn Nujaym, *Bahr al-Ra'iq*, 1:256.

[...continuing the 8 conditions of *tayammum*]

4. To completely wipe the parts required.[221]

5. To wipe the entire head or most of its part (*isti`ab al-mahall*).[222]

6. To strike the earth/soil with the inside of the palms twice.[223]

7. Suspending *tayammum* whenever anything precludes impurity (*hadath*), menstruation (*hayd*) as well as post-natal bleeding (*nifas*).[224]

8. Ensuring preventative barriers are removed from the skin (e.g. hard fatty greases, adhesives, wax, etc.).

---

[221] According to Imam al-Quduri wiping extends to (and includes) the elbows, *Mukhtasar*, p.12 (= *al-Lubab*, 1:52). See Abu Dawud, *Sunan* (#328) regarding this but which is deemed to have a weak chain. Narrations (#324-325) mention the narrator being unsure whether or not the Prophet wiped the hands or the elbows. Cf. Nasa'i, *Sunan* (#312 & 319) and Ibn Majah, *Sunan* (#570). However there are authentic narrations that state the Prophet wiped up to his shoulders (*ila 'l-manakib*), Abu Dawud, *Sunan* (#318 & 320) and Nasa'i, *Sunan* (#314).

[222] Meaning the 'face and hands.' The preposition ـِ / *ba* in the verse which reads: *wamsihu bi-wujuhikum* – 'and wipe your faces' is said by some to denote the partitive sense (*li 'l-tab`id*) thus meaning 'wipe part of your face.' The other reading is that the preposition is superfluous (*za'ida*) and thus renders the command as: 'wash [all] of your faces.' The opinion of the 4 *madhahib* Imams is that the entire face must be wiped.

[223] With the inner part of the palm of the hands (*bi-batin al-khuffayn*). After the first strike, one wipes the face and after the second strike, one wipes the arms up to (and including) the elbows. These are known as 'al-rukn' ('pillars/essentials') without which the action would be void; see al-Quduri, *Mukhtasar*, p. (= *al-Lubab*, 1:52) and al-Shurunbulali, *Maraqi al-Falah*, p.50.

[224] Meaning anything that incompatible with *tayammum* must discontinue before it can be be performed.

§3. The *sunna* aspects of *Tayammum*

1. Invocation of Allah's Name at the beginning (*tasmiyya*).

2. Following the sequence (*tartib*) shown by the Prophet (Allah bless him and grant him peace), e.g.

3. Performing the actions together without pauses or periods of rest (*mawalat*).

4. To rub the hands and arms back and forth (*iqbalan wa idbaran*).[225]

5. To shake the dust or earth off (*nafd*).[226]

6. To spread the fingers and brush them (*tafrij al-asabi`*).

---

[225] That is, with the earth or the material being used for *tayammum*. The Prophet also blew into his blessed hands (*nafakha fihima*) before performing it; see Bukhari, *Sahih* (#338).

[226] al-Nawawi, *Sharh Sahih Muslim*, p.411.

§4. That which invalidates *Tayammum*

- If water is found (*wajd al-ma'*) one may not perform *tayammum*.

- Every matter that invalidates the *wudu'* also invalidates the *tayammum* (e.g. gas, wind, urine, flowing blood, etc.).

- Every matter that invalidates the *ghusl* also invalidates the *tayammum* (e.g. sexual intercourse).

- *Tayammum* performed due to a disease is invalidated when one is cured from that disease.

- *Tayammum* performed due to a disability or ailment is invalidated when one has recovered from that disability or ailment.

§5. Additional Rulings related to *Tayammum*

- *Tayammum* can be performed before any prayer time.

- One can perform any number of prayers (*salah*) with one *tayammum* as long as it does not break.

- *Tayammum* performed for one obligatory (*fard*) Prayer will be valid for any extra (*nafl*) Prayer, for reading the Holy Qur'an, *Janaza* prayer, prostration for the recitation (*sajidat al-tilawa*), etc.

- One cannot do *tayammum* with water (i.e. half and half).

- If there is enough zam zam water available, then one may **not** perform *tayammum*.

- One cannot do *tayammum* on any wall, stone, mud, etc, if it had a stain on it and that stain dried up although *salah* would be permitted.

- The duration of *tayammum*, is as long as water is not available or the helplessness/inability to secure water continues even if this extends to months and years.

- Any wood, cloth or carpet that has a thick layer of dust on it such that a print remain upon touching it, one may use it for *tayammum*.

- Any prayers performed with *tayammum* do not have to be repeated once water is found.

- If there is no water and nothing with which one can perform *tayammum*, then one must perform an 'imitation prayer' going through the motions (*ruku`*, *sujud*, etc.) without intention and without reciting the

Qur'an. This prayer will have to be repeated however.[227]

- If one is extremely disabled (handicapped) he may perform *tayammum*.

- A sick or less able person may ask someone to perform the *tayammum* for them by rubbing their limbs for them on the condition that there be a clear intention made.[228] If the person making *tayammum* for the sick or less able person uses both his hands when wiping it over the limbs of that sick person then he will have to strike the object which he is using for *tayammum* three times. However, if the person making the *tayammum* only uses one hand, as in the case when making *tayammum* for one's self, then two strikes will be sufficient.[229]

---

[227] Ibn `Abidin, *Radd al-Muhtar*, 1:168.

[228] Ibn `Abidin, *Radd al-Muhtar*, 1:273:

فلو أمر غيره بأن ييممه جاز بشرط أن ينوي الآمر بحر قال ط ظاهره أنه يكفي من الغير ضربتان وهو خلاف ما يأتي عن القهستاني

[229] Ibn `Abidin, *Radd al-Muhtar*, 1:239:

نعم لو يمم غيره يضرب ثلاثا للوجه واليمنى واليسرى قهستاني

قوله (يضرب ثلاثا) أي لكل واحد من الأعضاء ضربة وهذا نقله القهستاني عن العماني وهو كتاب غريب والمشهور في الكتب المتداولة الإطلاق وهو الموافق للحديث الشريف التيمم ضربتان إلا أن يكون المراد إذا مسح يد المريض بكلتا يديه فحينئذ لا شبهة في أنه يحتاج إلى ضربة ثالثة يمسح بها يده الأخرى

SECTION 5: *MASH `ALA 'L-KHUFFAYN* ('WIPING OVER THE LEATHER SOCKS')

———— ◆ ————

Imam Hasan al-Basri said: "Seventy Companions of the Prophet related to me that the Messenger of Allah wiped over his leather socks (*masaha `ala'l-khuffayn*)...*"*[230]

حدثني سبعون أصحاب النبي (صلى الله عليه و سلم) أن رسول الله (صلى الله عليه و سلم) مسح على الخفين...

"[93] And we regard wiping over the leather socks as permitted for both the resident and the traveller...*"*[231]

[93] و نرى المسح على الخفين في الخضر و السفر...

- The primary texts used as a basis for this section are the well-known primers on Hanafi devotional injunctions entitled *al-Mukhtasar* ('The Abridged Legal Manual') of Imam al-Quduri and *Nur al-Idah* ('The Light of Clarification') by the Qadi of Egypt Imam al-Shurunbulali with his own interlinear commentary of the manual entitled *Maraqi al-Falah* ('The Ascent to Felicity').

§1. Preliminaries and Definitions

- Wiping is permitted in the Shari`a as it qualifies the general command to wash the feet for ritual performance of *wudu'*.

---

[230] Ibn Hajar al-`Asqalani, *Fath al-Bari*, 1:306.
[231] Shah `Abd al-Haqq al-Dihlawi, *Takmil al-Iman*, p.153.

- The Prophet wiped over his leather socks and his noble Companions too did this.[232]

- There is the consensus of all the Companions on its permissibility and denying it would be tantamount to blameworthy innovation.[233]

- The term 'mash' ('wiping') means something moist/wet that touches a surface or area.[234]

- There are specific types of footgear and they include the following:

  a. *Jawrab* (footgear made of cotton or wool [= *jukh*]).
  b. *Jurmuq* (regular boots worn over light leather boots).[235]
  c. *Mujallad* (footgear that has an upper and sole of leather).
  d. *Muna``al* (footgear with only the sole made of leather).
  e. *Khuff* (footgear made entirely of leather).

- It is permitted to wipe over all of the above except for the *jawrab* which is conditional upon meeting the following conditions:

---

[232] Bukhari, *Sahih* (#374) and Muslim, *Sahih* (#401).

[233] Ibn Hajar al-`Asqalani, *Fath al-Bari*, 1:305 and al-Marghinani, *al-Hidaya*, 1:30 (= English 1:53).

[234] Ibn `Abidin, *Radd al-Muhtar*, 1:67 and al-Kasani, *al-Bada'i` al-Sana'i`*, 1:171.

[235] al-Qal`aji, *Mu`jam Lughat al-Fuqaha'*, p.141. In al-Quduri's *Mukhtasar*, p.18 it has:

"The one who wears *jurmuq* over his leather socks may wipe over them." ومن لبس الجرموق فوق الخف مسح عليه.

a. It has to be made of a really thick material/fabric.

b. It must remain on the foot without being tied.

c. It must not be see-through and transparent.

d. It must completely cover the foot including the sides and ankles.

e. It can endure up to 3.5 miles of tension when one walks in it.

f. Water does not seep through when it is wiped.[236]

---

[236] See al-Shurunbulali, *Nur al-Idah*, pp.71-72; al-Sarakhsi, *Kitab al-Mabsut*, 1:18; Ibn al-Nujaym, *Bahr al-Ra'iq*, 1:191-192 and *al-Fatawa al-Hindiyya*, 1:32.

§2. Conditions for Wiping over the *Khuffayn*

- al-Shurunbulali states in *Nur al-Idah*:

"Conditions for the permissibility of wiping over the *khuffayn* are seven:

المسح على الخفين سبعة شروط الأول لبسهما بعد غسل الرجلين ولو قبل كمال الوضوء إذا أتمه قبل حصول ناقض للوضوء والثاني سترهما للكعبين والثالث إمكان متابعة المشي فيهما فلا يجوز على خف من زجاج أو خشب أو حديد والرابع خلو كل منهما عن خرق قدر ثلاث أصابع من أصغر أصابع القدم والخامس استمساكهما على الرجلين من غير شد والسادس منعهما وصول الماء الى الجسد والسابع أن يبقى من مقدم القدم قدر ثلاث أصابع من أصغر أصابع اليد فلو كان فاقدا مقدم قدمه لا يمسح على خفه ولو كان عقب القدم موجودا

[1] That they be worn after washing the feet, even though this be before completing the *wudu'*, as long as the *wudu'* is completed before the occurrence of anything that invalidates the *wudu'*. [2] The *khuff* must cover the ankle. [3] It should be possible to walk continuously in the *khuffayn*. It is however unlawful to wipe over *khuffayn* made of glass, wood or metal. [4] Each *khuff* must be free from any tear equivalent in size to the three smallest toes of the foot. [5] The *khuffayn* should cling to the feet without being tied and [6] prevent as well water from reaching the skin. [7] At least the equivalent of three of the smallest fingers of the hand from the front of the foot should exist, if this amount is absent then it is unlawful to wipe over the *khuff*, even though the heel of the foot exists.[237]

---

[237] al-Shurunbulali, *Nur al-Idah*, pp.71-72 and idem, *Maraqi al-Sa`adat*, p.53.

- In summary, the above conditions are:

a. The socks must be strong enough to enable walking in them on roads for approximately three miles without the socks tearing.

b. The socks should remain in position (covering the foreleg) without being tied. They should not slip. Socks which have elastic sewn into them (to keep them in position) will be regarded as being tied.

c. Water must not be able to seep through.

d. The socks must not be transparent or even semi-transparent.[238]

---

[238] *Talimul Haq*, pp.43-44.

§3. The Prophetic manner of Wiping over the *Khuffayn*

- Imam Ibn 'Abidin outlines the *sunna* manner of wiping:

"The *sunna* [s: manner of performing the ritual action of wiping] is to wipe (**in lines with the fingers**) of the hand (**spread out**) a little (**commencing from**) near (**the toes of the feet**) and moving in the direction (**towards**) the bottom (**of the shin** [s: = foreleg]). The area (**of the outer part of the leather socks**) encompasses the tips of the toes to its laces."[239]

والسنة أن يخطه (خطوطا بأصابع) يد) مفرجة) قليلا (يبدأ من) قبل (أصابع رجله) متوجها) إلى (أصل (الساق) ومحله (على ظاهر خفيه) من رءوس أصابعه إلى معقد الشراك.

- **Obligatory aspect**: A minimum extent of three small fingers is obligatory (*fard*) to wipe.

- The *masnun* (*sunna* way) way of performing the ritual act of wiping of the permitted footgear involves:

    1. Wiping once only on the top (not the side) section of the leather socks and not on the soles.

    2. After wetting the fingers, wiping should commence from the front, i.e. the toes.

    3. The fingers are placed flat on the footgear with the palms facing away from them.

---

[239] Ibn 'Abidin, *Radd al-Muhtar*, 1:497.

4. The left hand is used for the left foot and the right hand used for the right foot.

§4. Invalidators of Wiping

- Four factors invalidate the concession to wipe over the appropriate footgear, they include:

1. Anything that invalidates *wudu'* invalidates the application of wiping.

2. Removal of the footgear invalidates the concession to wipe.

3. When majority of one of the feet become wet, wiping is invalidated.

4. When the duration or period of time for wiping expires, wiping the footgear is no longer permitted, e.g. 24 hours for the resident and 72 hour for the traveller.

§5. Injunctions pertaining to Wiping

1. Wiping in general (e.g. for *wudu'*) may not be performed over the following:

   a. Face veils.
   b. Headscarf.
   c. Caps.
   d. Turbans.
   e. Gloves.
   f. Helmets.

2. The duration of wiping over the *khuffayn* is 24 hours (1 day and 1 night) for a resident and 72 hours (3 days and three nights) for a traveller. <u>The period of 24 or 72 hours will be reckoned from the time the *wudu'* (after which the *khuffayn* were put on) breaks, not from the time the *khuffayn* were put on.</u>

3. The time from which the permission to wipe commences is when one breaks h/her *wudu'*. If the *khuffayn* have been put on **before** a complete performance of *wudu'* has been made, then wiping over them **will not** be permissible. A complete *wudu'* has to be made then only should the *khuffayn* be put on. Thereafter if *wudu'* breaks, it will be permissible to over them without washing the feet when *wudu'* is being made.

4. It is not permissible to wipe over a *khuff* which is torn to such an extent that an area equal to the size of three small toes is exposed. It is permissible to wipe over the sock if it is torn less than this.

5. If the seam of the *khuff* comes loose, but while walking the foot is not exposed, wiping in this instance will be valid.

6. If a resident non-traveller (*muqim*) who has wiped over his leather socks goes on a journey before the expiry of 24 hours, the period of its validity will be extended to 72 hours. His permission to wipe will now be valid for 72 hours.

7. If a traveller (*musafir*) who has wiped over his *khuff* returns to his home town then the period of its validity will be reduced from 72 to 24 hours.

8. It is permissible to wipe over on ordinary woollen/cotton socks which have been covered with leather.

9. If *ghusl* becomes compulsory for a person, then wiping over the *khuffayn* **will not** be permissible even if the valid period has not yet expired. The *khuffayn* must be removed when the *ghusl* is performed and the feet washed.

10. If the back of the hand was used to make the wiping, it will be valid. However, one should not unnecessarily depart from the correct *Sunna* method.[240]

---

[240] Adapted from *Talimul Haq*, pp.43-44; al-Shurunbulali, *Nur al-Idah*, pp.73-74 and idem, *Maraqi al-Sa`adat*, pp.53-54.

SECTION SIX: QUESTIONS & ANSWERS: *TAHARA* ('PURITY')

———— ♦ ————

1] Ink and *Wudu'*

Q.

Salam * a brother said he had ink on his hand and it stained and was asking what the Hanafis say regarding whether his wudu will still be valid. Jzk**

A.

As far as I am aware, anything that prevents water from reaching the skin would mean the *wudu'* is invalid until that barrier is removed or eliminated. Of course, different inks have different levels or strengths of resistance so ball point inks are not the same as pigmented ink or indelible inks, etc. If the ink on his hand is from normal pens like ball points then it is porous or permeable (i.e. allows water to filter through it) and *wudu'* will be valid. In the *Maraqi al-Falah* it has:

"Whatever thing **prevents water** from reaching the body **like paste or dough** or wax or secretions from the eye that solidify and prevent anything entering then **one must** – i.e. he is obligated to – **wash it** after removing it..."[241]	(ما) أي شيء (يمنع الماء) أن يصل إلى الجسد (كعجين) وشمع ورمص بخارج العين بتغميضها (وجب) أي افترض (غسل ما تحته) بعد إزالة المانع...

And Allah knows best.

––––––––––––––––––––

[241] Imam al-Shurunbulali, *Maraqi al-Falah*, p.63. The text in bold is that of *Nur al-Idah*.

2] Waxing and Shaving the Body

Q. Bro are we allowd [*sic.*] to shave or wax our chest hairs?

A.

Yes, although I have heard that there is some element of dislike in it. In the *Radd al-Muhtar* of Imam Ibn `Abidin, it has:

"There is no harm in shaving hair from the chest or the back...[242]

...ولا بأس في حلق شعر الصدر والظهر

And Allah knows best.

3] Wiping over Socks

Q. I get confused. Can we wipe over socks or not? I get different people telling me different things.

A.

There are specific types of footgear that are mentioned in the *fiqh* books and they include amongst others, the following:

f. *Jawrab* (footgear made of cotton or wool [= *jukh*]).[243]

g. *Jurmuq* (regular boots worn over light leather boots).[244]

---

[242] Ibn `Abidin, *Radd al-Muhtar*, 6:407. See also Mawlana Ashraf Ali Thanvi's, *Beheshti Zewar*, p.830.

[243] See al-Mubarakpuri, *Tuhfat al-Ahwadhi*, 1:281-282 for a list of meanings.

    h. *Mujallad* (footgear that has an upper and sole of leather).

    i. *Muna``al* (footgear with only the sole made of leather).

    j. *Khuff* (footgear made entirely of leather).

It is permitted to wipe over all of the above except for the *jawrab* which is conditional upon meeting the following conditions:

    g. It has to be made of a really thick material/fabric.

    h. It must remain on the foot without being tied.

    i. It must not be see-through and transparent.

    j. It must completely cover the foot including the sides and ankles.

    k. It can endure up to 3.5 miles of tension when one walks in it.

    l. Water does not seep through when it is wiped.[245]

Imam Ibn `Abidin in his commentary on Imam al-Haskafi's *Durr al-Mukhtar* writes regarding this issue:

Regarding his statement (**even if it is made out of wool or hair [s: of animals]**). What is included in this is *jukh* as was

(قوله ولو من غزل أو شعر) دخل فيه الجوخ كما حققه في شرح المنية. وقال

---

[244] al-Qal`aji, *Mu`jam Lughat al-Fuqaha'*, p.141. In al-Quduri's *Mukhtasar*, p.18 it has:

"The one who wears *jurmuq* over his leather socks may wipe over them."

ومن لبس الجرموق فوق الخف مسح عليه.

[245] See al-Shurunbulali, *Nur al-Idah*, pp.71-72; al-Sarakhsi, *Kitab al-Mabsut*, 1:18 and idem *al-Bada'i` al-Sana'i`*, 1:83; Ibn al-Nujaym, *Bahr al-Ra'iq*, 1:191-192 and *al-Fatawa al-Hindiyya*, 1:32.

verified in *Sharh al-Munya*. And he said: what is not included is anything made from *kirbas* – with a *kasra* – which is a coarse cloth made from white cotton. And he also included with the *kirbas* anything that is made of thread such as *al-kitan and al-ibrisam* [s: a kind of pure unwoven silk) and other similar things to them. In the marginalia of Imam al-Halabi on the *Durr al-Mukhtar* [ح] he suspended judgment over the non-permissibility of wiping over them if the four conditions mentioned by the commentator were found. I say: what is apparent is that if the conditions are met, then it is permitted to wipe over them. It may be that the scholars excluded them from it because they did not fulfil most of the conditions and this is suggested in the *Kafy* of al-Nasafi where he justified the impermissibility of wiping over socks made of *kirbas* because one could not continuously walk in them which suggests that if it *was* possible, then he would permit wiping over it. What is also indicated is that which is mentioned in the marginalia of Imam al-Tahtawi on the *Durr al-Mukhtar* [ط] from *al-*

: وخرج عنه ما كان من كرباس بالكسر: وهو الثوب من القطن الأبيض؛ ويلحق بالكرباس كل ما كان من نوع الخيط كالكتان والإبريسم ونحوهما. وتوقف ح في وجه عدم جواز المسح عليه إذا وجد فيه الشروط الأربعة التي ذكرها الشارح. وأقول : الظاهر أنه إذا وجدت فيه الشروط يجوز، وأنهم أخرجوه لعدم تأتي الشروط فيه غالبا، يدل عليه ما في كافي النسفي حيث علل جواز المسح على الجورب من كرباس بأنه لا يمكن تتابع المشي عليه، فإنه يفيد أنه لو أمكن جاز، ويدل عليه أيضا ما في ط عن الخانية أن كل ما كان في معنى الخف في إدمان المشي عليه وقطع السفر به ولو من لبد رومي يجوز المسح عليه . ١ ه

Khaniyya that whatever is in the meaning of a *khuff* where one is able to walk continuously in it or undertake a journey with it even if it was byzantine wool (*labad rumi*), it would be permitted to wipe over it."[246]

"Regarding his statement (**thick and coarse**) means that footgear which is not leather nor is the sole made of leather [...] as for the conditions of something being a *khuff*, it was mentioned by the commentator earlier at the beginning of the section. Like [the khuff] is the *jurmuq* because of the fact that it is made in most part from leather [...] His statement regarding (**can last a walk for 1** *farsakh* [s: approximately three miles in distance]) can mean more as already mentioned [...] (by itself) i.e. without it being tied [ط] (**without it ripping or tearing**) [...] such that one can see what is underneath it [...]".[247]

(قوله على الثخينين) أي اللذين ليسا مجلدين ولا منعلين نهر، وهذا التقييد مستفاد من عطف ما بعده عليه، وبه يعلم أنه نعت للجوربين فقط كما هو صريح عبارة الكنز. وأما شروط الخف فقد ذكرها أول الباب، ومثله الجرموق ولكونه من الجلد غالبا لم يقيده بالثخانة المفسرة بما ذكره الشارح؛ لأن الجلد الملبوس لا يكون إلا كذلك عادة (قوله بحيث يمشي فرسخا) أي فأكثر كما مر، وفاعل يمشي ضمير يعود على الجورب والإسناد إليه مجازي، أو على اللابس له والعائد محذوف أي به (قوله بنفسه) أي من

[246] Ibn `Abidin, *Radd al-Muhtar*, 1:269.
[247] Ibn `Abidin, *Radd al-Muhtar*, 1:269.

غير شد ط (قوله ولا يشف) بتشديد

الفاء، من شف الثوب : رق حتى رأيت ما

وراءه، من باب ضرب مغرب. وفي بعض

الكتب : ينشف بالنون قبل الشين، من

نشف الثوب العرق كسمع ونصر شربه

قاموس، والثاني أولى هنا لئلا يتكرر مع

قوله تبعا للزيلعي ولا يرى ما تحته، لكن

فسر في الخانية الأولى بأن لا يشف

الجورب الماء إلى نفسه كالأديم والصرم،

وفسر الثاني بأن لا يجاوز الماء إلى القدم

وكأن تفسيره الأول مأخوذ من قولهم

اشتف ما في الإناء شربه كله كما في

القاموس، وعليه فلا تكرار فافهم...قال

الرافعي : (لا يشف الجورب الماء الى

نفسه) أى ماء المسح لا ماء الغسل كما

فى الامداد.

- Imam al-Tahtawi in his glosses on the *Maraqi al-Falah* writes:

"(From something coarse and thick) know that the issue (من شيء ثخين) اعلم أن المسئلة على

pertaining to *khuffs* has three aspects: if they are thin without leathered soles, it will not be permitted to wipe over them according to agreement of all the scholars. If they are thick, coarse and with leathered sole then it will be permitted to wipe over them according to agreement of all the scholars. However, if they are thick and coarse and are not leathered in their soles then they are a point of disagreement ad mentioned in *al-Khaniyya*... **(and that water does not seep through)** i.e. water does not reach the feet as mentioned in *al-Khaniyya* [...]"[248]

ثلاثة وجوه إن كانا رقيقين غير منعلين لا يجوز المسح عليهما إتفاقا وإن كانا ثخينين منعلين جاز إتفاقا وإن كان ثخينين غير منعلين فهو محل الإخلاف كما في الخانية...(لا يشف الماء) أي لا يتجاوز منه الماء إلى القدم ذكره في الخانية... (وإليه رجع الإمام) أي قبل موته بثلاثة أيام وقيل بسبعة وذلك أنه مسح على جوربيه في مرضه ثم قال لعودة : فعلت ما كنت أمنع الناس عنه فاستدلوا بذلك على رجوعه كما في البدائع و التبيين...

With regard to modern nylon and cotton socks, it would not be permitted to wipe over them as they do not fulfil the conditions required for wiping.

And Allah knows best.

---

[248] See al-Tahtawi*'s Hashiyat* on *Maraqi al-Falah*, p.138.

4] *Wudu'* and Cleaning Nappies

Q. I have a new born child and like any new dad have to clean the nappies. Would my wudu break if i touch the babies [*sic.*] urine and poo?

A.

Urine and faeces is of course considered impure categories of substances but of that kind which if washed, the impurity is considered removed. It does not however invalidate the *wudu'*. Imam al-Shurunbulali states:

"And filth regardless of whether it is on the body, clothes or utensils is **purified** even if it is heavy filth **and visible** – like blood – by <u>removing the filth itself</u> **even if it is achieved by washing it once. This is the correct view.** Repeated washing is not a condition because the filth itself is what is considered so one can stop when it disappears..."[249]	(ويطهر متنجس) سواء كان بدنا أو ثوبا أو آنية (بنجاسة) ولو غليظة (مرئية) كدم (بزوال عينها ولو)كان بمرة) أي غسلة واحدة (على الصحيح) ولا يشترط التكرار لأن النجاسة فيه باعتبار عينها فتزول بزوالها...

Thus, if any of the baby's urine of faeces comes into contact with your hand all that would be required is to wash it off with water.

And Allah knows best.

---

[249] al-Shurunbulali, *Maraqi al-Falah*, p.64.

5] *Wudu'* and Breastfeeding

Q. I just had a new baby girl and my wife is breastfeeding her. My mother-in-law said that she should do her wadu again after breastfeeding the baby. Is this correct?

A.

Breastfeeding does not contravene the *wudu'*.

And Allah knows best.

6] *Wudu'* and Digital Qur'ans

Q. Salam * what do know about touch screen Qurans? Do we have to have wudu for it? Ws**

A.

It must first be remembered that the Noble Qur'an is the inimitable word of Allah (swt) and the *fuqaha'* (Muslim jurists) have written much on the etiquettes (*adab*) of handling (*haml*) and reciting (*tilawa*) of the Qur'an. We must take the utmost care reciting it observing these etiquettes out of humility and complete love for it.

No doubt, the common mode of Qur'an recitation is from a standard printed edition (i.e. in book form) but there has increasingly emerged electronic *mushafs* or entire Qur'ans scanned on to digital computer programs the same being the case with iPod and iPhones or any memory capacity on mobile phones. As far as I am aware and presently know (which is extremely limited), *wudu'* would be required to touch the screen e.g. when scrolling or turning over a digital page. In Imam al-Tahtawi's *Hashiya* on al-Shurunbulali's *Maraqi al-Falah* it has:

"Likewise, *wudu'* is *fard*[250] for touching the *Mushaf* even if it is a verse etched on a coin or wall based on His (Mighty and Exalted) statement (*none but the purified shall touch it...*)[251] – the same being paper and the blank areas (margins). Some of our teachers consider it disliked for the one in ritual impurity to touch the area that it is written without the commentary because he is not in actual fact touching the Qur'an. However, the correct position is that touching it is like touching what is written."[252]

كذا الوضوء فرض (لمس المصحف ولو آية) مكتوبة على درهم أو حائط لقوله تعالى " لا يمسه إلا المطهرون " وسواء الكتابة والبياض وقال بعض مشايخنا إنما يكره للمحدث مس الموضع المكتوب دون الحواشي لأنه لم يمس القرآن حقيقة والصحيح أن مسها كمس المكتوب...

So, any form of the Qur'an being written, recorded or etched (which would include digital texts of the Qur'an) will require the etiquette of performing *wudu'*. For clarification it would be better to ask your local Imam about it.

And Allah knows best.

---

[250] The word "fard" here means what has been established with definitive evidence. al-Shurunbulali, *Maraqi al-Falah*, p.34.
[251] *Surat* al-Waqi`a:79.
[252] al-Shurunbulali, *Maraqi al-Falah*, p.34.

7] Using only Toilet Paper

Q. Can we use the public toilets that only have toilet paper?

A.

The toilets here in London of course do not have facilities that make cleansing easy and efficient. Indeed, it is not the norm here in the West to wash the rear area after going to the toilet. If after relieving oneself one should clean the effected area by either 1) washing the area (assisted with any material like toilet paper) or 2) using only toilet paper. Ideal will be to use toilet paper and water together and the least ideal would be to use only toilet paper. However, anyone of these modes of cleaning the affected area will fulfil the requirement of the *sunna* of *istinja'* (albeit with varying grades of reward) and **does not** affect the validity of the Prayer, i.e. one will still be considered ritually pure (*tahir*) if say only tissue was used to clean the area. This is the case if the size of impurity around the affected area is less than a coin.

In the legal commentary *al-Lubab* ('The Essence') of the classical Hanafi manual of law (*fiqh*) *Mukhtasar* of Imam al-Quduri, Imam al-Ghunaymi, states:

"And it is stated in the *Lubab*: **and performing al-istinja' is sunna** *mu'akkada* for men and women." Using stones or anything in place of it **will suffice** [...] **one wipes it** i.e. the area **until it is cleaned** because the aim is to be clean [...] **if the filth exceeds its orifice then only**	قال في اللباب: (والاستنجاء سنة) مؤكدة للرجال والنساء، (يجزئ فيه) لإقامة السنة (الحجر وما قام مقامه) من كل عين طاهرة قالعة غير محترمة ولا متقومة كمدر (يمسحه) أي: المخرج (حتى ينقيه)، لأن المقصود

water may be used...”[253]

هو الإنقاء، فيعتبر ما هو المقصود ... (وبعد أسطر) ... (فإن تجاوزت النجاسة مخرجها) وكان المتجاوز بانفراده — لسقوط اعتبار ذلك الموضع — أكثر من الدرهم (لم يجز فيه) أي: في طهارته (إلا الماء)، أو المائع، ولا يطهر بالحجر ، لأنه من باب إزالة النجاسة الحقيقية عن البدن ...

- In the encyclopaedic work of Hanafi law by Imam Ibn `Abidin, it has:

“Then also know that combining water and stones is better followed by water only and then stones only. However, the *sunna* will be fulfilled by all despite being different in excellence as mentioned in *al-Imdad* and other [works]...”[254]

وقال في حاشية ابن عابدين: ثم اعلم أن الجمع بين الماء والحجر أفضل، ويليه في الفضل الاقتصار على الماء، ويليه الاقتصار على الحجر وتحصل السنة بالكل وإن تفاوت الفضل كما أفاده في الإمداد وغيره....

And Allah knows best.

---

[253] al-Ghunaymi, *al-Lubab fi Sharh al-Kitab*, pp.55-56. The text of Imam al-Quduri is in bold.
[254] Ibn `Abidin, *Radd al-Muhtar*, 1:60.

8] *Wudu'* and Islamic Books

Q. Salam bro, our books have fiqh sections and tafseer sections with the Arabic verses do we have to have wudu to read those areas and touch them? Also, what about books of hadeeth, do we have to have wudu for them as well?

A.

According to a known position in the School of Imam Abu Hanifa (ra): i) it is not permitted to touch the Qur'an without performing *wudu'* ('ritual ablution'); ii) it is not permitted (or extremely disliked)[255] to even touch a translation of the Qur'an without *wudu'*;[256] iii) if the *fiqh*

---

[255] Ibn al-Nizam et al, *al-Fatawa al-Hindiyya*, 1:39:

"If the Qur'an is written in the Persian language it is disliked to touch it according to Abu Hanifa and likewise according to [Abu Yusuf and al-Shaybani] according to the most correct position as mentioned in *al-Khulasa...*"

ولو كان القرآن مكتوبا بالفارسية يكره لهم مسه عند أبي حنيفة وكذا عندهما على الصحيح هكذا في الخلاصة...

[256] al-Shurunbulali, *Maraqi al-Falah*, p.82:

"...even if it is in the Persian Language it is not permitted to touch it by agreement according to the correct position..."

كذا الوضوء فرض (لمس القرآن ولو آية) مكتوبة على درهم أو حائط لقوله تعالى: {لا يمسه إلا المطهرون} وسواء الكتابة والبياض ، وقال بعض مشائخنا: إنما يكره للمحدث مس الموضع المكتوب دون الحواشي لأنه لم يمس القرآن حقيقة والصحيح إن مسها كمس المكتوب ، ولو بالفارسية يحرم مسه اتفاقا على الصحيح...

text, *tafsir* text or *hadith* text has more Qur'anic than non-Qur'anic material, then *wudu'* would be required otherwise not and iv) it is highly recommended (*mandub*) to perform *wudu'* before reading books of law, doctrine and *hadith*, known as *al-kutub al-shar'iyya* ('Islamic books'), out of respect (*ta'zim*) for them.[257]

And Allah knows best.

9] Shaving Private Parts

Q. If we have to shave our private parts does this mean hair on the rear end? And isnt that a bit difficult?

A.

As far as I know, the noble *fuqaha'* have stated that 1) hair on the actual private part; 2) hair around the private part and 3) hair above the private part ought to be removed. This therefore includes hair from the scrotum. In the *Maraqi al-Falah* it states:

"It is highly recommended to ويستحب إزالة شعر الدبر خوفا من أن
remove hair from the backside
out of fear that any filth

---

[257] al-Shurunbulali, *Maraqi al-Falah*, p.82:

(و) القسم (الثالث) وضوء (مندوب) في أحوال كثيرة كمس الكتب الشرعية، ورخص مسها للمحدث إلا

التفسير قوله (كمس الكتب الشرعية) نحو الفقه، والحديث، والعقائد، فيتطهر لها تعظيما ...

"... (**and**) part (**three**) is that *wudu'* (**is recommended**) in many situations such as touching shari'a books; there being dispensation for the *muhaddith* to touch it except *tafsir* works. His statement (**like touching shari'a books**) like *fiqh*, *hadith*, 'aqa'id etc. in this case purification is made out of respect for them..."

coming out will attach itself to it...[258] ...يعلق به شيء من النجاسة الخارجة

From this, it would mean that if it is not too difficult for someone to do, then any hair that can be removed that is located between the penis and anus must be removed.

And Allah knows best.

10] *Wudu'* and Hair Gels

Q. slm *** is it permitted to do wudu with hair gel?

A.

I take it you mean to perform *wudu'* while having gel already applied on the hair? As far as I know the *wudu'* will be valid as long as it is not so thick as to prevent water from reaching the hair:

"And his statement (**the same applies if he applies any oil**) like oil or lubricants and sesame oil different from grease or solid fat. His statement (*al-dasuma* [s: a type of fatty grease]) is the remains of the oil as mentioned by al-Shurunbulali. al-Maqdisi said: In *al-Fatawa* it mentions, 'he applied oil to his feet and then performed *wudu'* and [thereafter] poured [water] across his legs and water did

قوله و كذا دهن اى كزيت و شيرج بخلاف نحو شحم و سمن جامد قوله و دسومة هى اثر الدهن قال فى الشرنبلالية قال المقدسى : و فى الفتاوى دهن رجليه ثم توضأ و امرّ على رجليه و لم يقبل الماء للدسومة جاز لوجود غسل الرجلين...

---

[258] al-Shurunbulali, *Maraqi al-Falah*, p.527.

not reach [the required area] due to the oil'. This is permitted due to the feet being washed...[259]

"My father, may Allah Most High have mercy on him, said that if one applies oil to his feet and then pours water and it does not reach [the skin] due to the oily area, *wudu'* is still permitted as mentioned in *Khazanat al-Fatawa*. In *Majmu` al-Nawazil* it has: washing requires pouring water over the parts without it sticking. If he oils those parts of the body required for *wudu'* and then pours water over them and it does not stick to the skin, then it is permitted..."[260]

قال والدى رحمه الله تعالى اذا دهن رجليه و امرّ الماء و لم يصل لمكان الدسومات جاز الوضوء كما فى خزانة الفتاوى و فى مجموع النوازل: الغسل يقتضى جواز اسالة الماء على الاعضاء دون الازاق فلو دهن اعضاء الوضوء ثم سال عليها الملء و لم يلتزق عليها جاز...

As a rule, anything that prevents water from reaching the skin with a barrier will not render *wudu'* valid until that barrier is removed.

And Allah knows best.

---

[259] Ibn `Abidin, *Radd al-Muhtar*, 1:154.
[260] al-Ghunaymi, *Nihayat al-Murad*, p.81.

11] *Wudu'* and Urine Drops

Q. If we go to the toilet and then after that do wudhu but still some urine drops accidentally come out is our wudhu and prayer still valid?

A.

With regards to the accidental emission of urine drops on one's clothes or underwear, if the size of the impurity is larger than a dirham (approximately 5cm) then if one prayed without washing that affected area of impurity then the prayer (*salah*) would still be valid but will also be *makruh* (disliked). It would thus be preferable for the size of the affected area to be washed and removed including washing the private parts.[261]

---

[261] See Ibn Nujaym, *al-Bahr al-Ra'iq*, 1:228:

ومراده من العفو صحة الصلاة بدون إزالته لا عدم الكراهة لما في السراج الوهاج وغيره إن كانت النجاسة قدر

الدرهم تكره الصلاة معها إجماعا، وإن كانت أقل وقد دخل في الصلاة نظر إن كان في الوقت سعة فالأفضل

إزالتها واستقبال الصلاة، وإن كانت تفوته الجماعة، فإن كان يجد الماء ويجد جماعة آخرين في موضع آخر

فكذلك أيضا ليكون مؤديا للصلاة الجائزة بيقين، وإن كان في آخر الوقت أو لا يدرك الجماعة في موضع آخر

يمضي على صلاته ولا يقطعها ...

والظاهر أن الكراهة تحريمية لتجويزهم رفض الصلاة لأجلها ولا ترفض لأجل المكروه تنزيها وسوى في فتح

القدير بين الدرهم وما دونه في الكراهة ورفض الصلاة، وكذا في النهاية والمحيط وفي الخلاصة ما يقتضي

الفرق بينهما فإنه قال : وقدر الدرهم لا يمنع ويكون مسيئا، وإن كان أقل فالأفضل أن يغسلها ولا يكون مسيئا

. ا هـ

Other possible references include Mahmud al-Hasan al-Gangohi, *Fatawa al-Mahmudiyya*, 5:222; Rashid Ahmed Ludhianvi, *Ahsan al-Fatawa*, 2:89 and Ashraf Ali Thanvi, *Beheshti Zewar*, 2:2.

And Allah knows best.

12] Waxing the Body

Q. Someone said that waxing is absolutely haraam because he asked a scholar and he said it was not allowed as it is like changing the creation of Allah. What do you think?

A.

I'm not a scholar but the opinion as far as I know in the school of Imam Abu Hanifa (may Allah be pleased with him) is that it is permitted but perhaps with dislike (*karaha*) as mentioned in one place in *al-Fatawa al-Hindiyya*:

"...and in shaving the chest and back hair is abandoning etiquette as mentioned in *al-Qaniyya* but if one treats the pubic area with a depilatory agent it is permitted as mentioned in *al-Ghara'ib* [262]..."	وفي حلق شعر الصدر والظهر ترك الأدب كذا في القنية ولو عالج بالنورة في العانة يجوز كذا في الغرائب ...

I'm not too sure if waxing or shaving is changing the creation of Allah. If it was considered that severe then I'm sure the Hanafi jurists would have mentioned that point and thus declared the action *haram* ('unlawful'). Nevertheless, it is not a requirement neither is it recommended hence if one so wishes then they may without blame wax themselves. This also includes shaving or waxing of the legs and the permissibility of another to apply the shaving or waxing procedure.[263]

---

[262] See *al-Fatawa al-Hindiyya*, 5:358.
[263] See *al-Fatawa al-Hindiyya*, 5:358:

And Allah knows best.

13] Nail Polish and Prayer

Q. is nail-polish halal and is it allowed tp [sic] pray with it?

A.

I believe that if the nail-polish does not contain unlawful constituents, it is permitted. As for performing the *salah* with it on, then it would not be permitted because it would fail to fulfil a condition of *wudu'*, namely: if a barrier prevents water from reaching the body or skin, then unless that barrier is removed, *wudu'* will be invalid. In the *Maraqi al-Falah* it has:

"**Whatever** thing **prevents water** from reaching the body **like paste or dough** or wax or secretions from the eye that solidify and prevent anything entering then **one must** – i.e. he is obligated to – **wash it** after removing it..."[264]

(ما) أي شيء (يمنع الماء) أن يصل إلى الجسد (كعجين) وشمع ورمص بخارج العين بتغميضها (وجب) أي افترض (غسل ما تحته) بعد إزالة المانع...

Nail-polish contains film forming agents, resins and plasticizers, solvents, and coloring agents that form an adhesive sticking to the nails. This becomes a barrier that prevents water (i.e. it is impermeable). Thus, for prayer

---

في جامع الجوامع حلق عانته بيده وحلق الحجام جائز إن غض بصره كذا في التتارخانية...

[264] al-Shurunbulali, *Maraqi al-Falah*, p.63. The text in bold is that of *Nur al-Idah*.

purposes, nail-polish cannot be worn. It may be worn after completion of the Prayer.

And Allah knows best.

14] *Wudu'* and Partial Emission

Q. Does wudu break even without full release from the guy?

A.

- In *al-Fatawa al-Hindiyya* it has the following statements:

"...if a man urinates and then secretes semen (*mani*) then he must perform the full bath (*al-ghusl*) if it was from an erection and if it was not then he must perform the *wudu'* as mentioned in *al-Khulasa*..."

رجل بال فخرج من ذكره مني إن كان منتشرا عليه الغسل وإن كان منكسرا عليه الوضوء . كذا في الخلاصة .

"...In *al-Durr al-Mukhtar* it has: and (**it is obligatory**) to perform the *ghusl* only (**after**) (**semen**) has been emitted from the body by agreement because it falls under the ruling of the inconspicuous (**released from its place**) which is the semen of the man and the fluid of the woman. The semen from men is whitish in colour whereas the ejaculatory fluid of women is

في الدر المختار: (وفرض) الغسل (عند) خروج (مني) من العضو وإلا فلا يفرض اتفاقا؛ لأنه في حكم الباطن (منفصل عن مقره) هو صلب الرجل وترائب المرأة، ومنيه أبيض ومنيها أصفر، فلو اغتسلت فخرج منها مني، وإن منيها أعادت الغسل لا الصلاة وإلا لا) بشهوة

yellowish in colour. If she washes the area and ejaculatory fluid is actually released then she must repeat the *ghusl* but not any Prayers otherwise there is no [repetition] (**if it is through desire**) meaning pleasure even though it carries the same ruling of one who has a wet dream..."[265]

أي لذة ولو حكما كمحتلم...)

و في الشامية : (قوله: بشهوة) متعلق بقوله منفصل، احترز به عما لو انفصل بضرب أو حمل ثقيل على ظهره، فلا غسل عندنا خلافا للشافعي كما في الدرر...

"And in the *Shamiyya* (**his saying: out of pleasure**) is connected to his statement of secretion or release. He has cautioned in that if he secreted or released by being struck or carrying a heavy load on his back, then there is no *ghusl* for him according to our position in opposition to the Shafi`is as mentioned in *al-Durar*..."[266]

Allah knows best.

15] Bandages/Wounds and *Wudu'*

Q. Bandage over a wound and wudu'.

A.

---

[265] See al-Haskafi, *al-Durr al-Muktar*, 1:325.
[266] See Ibn `Abidin, *Radd al-Muhtar*, 1:326. See also the *Hashiyat* of Imam al-Tahtawi on the *Maraqi al-Falah*, p.61 and *al-Fatawa al-Hindiyya*, 1:14.

If you have a wound and it is wrapped in a plain bandage, cloth or medical bandage then you must see if you are able to unwind the bandage and wash the wounded area when performing *wudu'*. However, if you are unable due to the severity of the wound (or if you are in a plaster), then you may leave the bandage as it is and wipe over the greater part of the bandage (perhaps more than half)[267] and this will suffice. Hanafi manuals contain the following rulings regarding this particular *mas'ala*:

"If a limb has either broken or is wounded and has been tied with a cloth or a splint and one is unable to either wash the limb or wipe it, then he must make mash (wiping) over most of the cloth [or	إذا افتصد أو جرح أو كسر عضوه فشده بخرقة أو جبيرة وكان لا يستطيع غسل العضو ولا يستطيع مسحه وجب المسح

---

[267] See for example al-Baydawi's *Tawali` al-Anwar*, p.324; al-Halabi, *Ghunyat al-Mutamalli fi Sharh Munyat al-Musalli*, p.117 and *al-Fatawa al-Hindiyya*, 2:35:

"It is obligatory when making mash to wipe the extent of three fingers although there is disagreement over wiping over a bandage or splint. Some have said the entire bandage or splint must be wiped over, others have said half and yet others most of it..."	ان المفروض في مسح الخف قدر ثلاث اصبع واختلف في مسح الجبيرة فقيل كلها وقيل نصفها وقيل اكثرها...
"some have said it is permitted to wipe over most of the [bandage or splint] and the author of *al-Hidaya* inclines to this position..."	(قالوا اذا مسح على اكثرها جاز) واليه مال صاحب الهداية...
"it suffices to wipe over a large part of the bandage or splint as mentioned in *al-Hidaya*..."	ويكتفي بالمسح على أكثر الجبيرة هكذا في الهداية ...

bandage]."[268]

على أكثر ما شد به العضو...

"It suffices to wipe over most of the bandage..."[269]

ويكفي المسح على أكثر العصابة...

"(and if one is unable to cleanse [the wound] he must make wiping) according to the most correct opinion once or repeatedly except if it is the head ... some have said it is obligatory (*fard*) because the Prophet used to wipe over his bandage [...] and the author of *al-Kanz* has preferred that one wipes over the entire bandage..."[270]

(ولا يستطيع مسحه وجب المسح) على

الصحيح مرة واحدة في الصحيح وقيل

يكرر إلا في الرأس واستحبابه رواية وقيل

فرض لأن النبي صلى الله عليه و سلم كان

يمسح على عصابته ولما كسر زند علي

رضي الله تعالى عنه يوم أحد أو يوم خيبر

أمره النبي صلى الله عليه و سلم أن يمسح

على الجبائر ويمسح (على أكثر ما شد به

العضو) هو الصحيح لئلا يؤدي إلى فساد

الجراحة بالاستيعاب... قال الإمام

الطحطاوي في حاشيته: (وهو الصحيح)

وفي التتمة به يفتي وفي الخلاصة، وعليه

الفتوى، وإليه جنح صاحب الهداية واختار

في الكنز الاستيعاب...

[268] al-Shurunbulali, *Nur al-Idah*, p.47.
[269] al-Ghunaymi, *Nihayat al-Murad fi Sharh Hadiyat Ibn al-`Imad*, p.399.
[270] al-Tahtawi, *Hashiyat 'ala Maraqi al-Falah*, p.135.

"And the Qadi and Imam Abu `Ali al-Husayn b. al-Khidr al-Nasafi (Allah have mercy on him) says that wiping over a splint, bandage or cloth is permitted when one is unable to clear the wound or if it is infected and when one is unable to wash it because the water will harm him. If he is able to wipe and wash the wound or infection then he is not permitted to wipe over the bandage or cloth..."[271]

وكان القاضي الإمام أبو علي الحسين بن الخضر النسفي رحمه الله يقول: المسح على الجبائر إنما يجوز إذا كان لا يقدر على القرحة كما كان لا يقدر على غسلها بأن كان يضرها الماء، أما إذا كان يقدر على القرحة على المسح لا يجوز المسح على الجبائر، كما لو كان قادراً على غسلها، فلم يغسلها وكان يقول ينبغي أن يحفظ هذا، فإن الناس عن هذا غافلون

...

"It is permitted to wipe over a cloth or splint above a wound...

ثم إذا مسح على الجبائر، والخرق التي فوق الجراحة جاز...

If one unties a bandage and washes the wounded area under it and it harms the wound then it is permitted to make *mash* (wiping) on the remaining part of the bandage and the wiping over takes the place of washing what is under it like wiping over the bandage that touches the wound. If it does not harm the wound by untying the bandage and washing the

ينظر إن كان حل الخرقة، وغسل ما تحتها من حوالي الجراحة مما يضر بالجرح يجوز المسح على الخرقة الزائدة، ويقوم المسح عليها مقام غسل ما تحتها كالمسح على الخرقة التي تلاصق الجراحة، وإن كان ذلك لا يضر بالجرح عليه أن يحل،

---

[271] al-Bukhari, *al-Muhit al-Burhani*, 1:360.

wounded area, then it would not be permitted to make mash because the permission is based on necessity (*al-darura*) so one acts according to what one is able according to necessity.

The same condition also applies to splints [...]"[272]

ويغسل حوالي الجراحة، ولا يجوز المسح عليها؛ لأن الجواز لمكان الضرورة فيقدر بقدر الضرورة ...

ومن شرط جواز المسح على الجبيرة أيضا أن يكون المسح على عين الجراحة مما يضر بها، فإن كان لا يضر بها لا يجوز المسح إلا على نفس الجراحة، ولا يجوز على الجبيرة، كذا ذكره الحسن بن زياد؛ لأن الجواز على الجبيرة للعذر، ولا عذر...

And Allah knows best.

16] *Wudu'* after Ghusl

Q. Wudu after ghusl.

A.

If the obligatory aspects of the *ghusl* (the full purificatory bath) are made, then one will not be required to

---

[272] al-Kasani, *al-Bada'i` al-Sana'i*, 1:130 f.

perform *wudu'* again after it although in the Hanafi *madhhab*, it is *sunna* to do so.[273]

And Allah knows best.

17] Droplets of urine after Using the Toilet

Q. Droplets of urine after using the toilet.

A.

Droplets of urine after visiting the toilet can remain or seep out long after. There is a process of ensuring droplets of urine or residue is extracted called *istibra* and is highly recommended. One procedure involves using the middle finger and/or index finger of the left hand pressing down upon the urethra starting from between the scrotum and the anus moving forward along the penis forcing any urine drops. This can be helped if tissue is used to catch the droplets so as to avoid any droplets falling on one's clothes. Another way perhaps to force droplets out is by coughing a few times.

"...{just like how} there is no nullification {if one inserts or dabs his urethra with cotton and moistens the outer part} this being the case if the cotton is high up or facing the tip of the urethra whereas if it is at the bottom of it, then it does not nullify. The same ruling holds for the anus, private parts and {if one moistens} the interior

كما) ينقض لو حشا إحليله بقطنة وابتل الطرف الظاهر) هذا لو القطنة عالية أو محاذية لرأس الإحليل وإن متسفلة عنه لا ينقض وكذا الحكم في الدبر والفرج الداخل (وإن ابتل) الطرف

---

[273] See al-Shurunbulali, *Maraqi al-Falah*, p.58 and Ashraf Ali Thanwi, *Behesti Zewar*, p.51.

part then there is no nullification..."[274]

الداخل لا ينقض...

Allah knows best.

18] Cleaning between the Toes

Q. When do we clean between the toes. I thought it was while we were doing wudu.

A.

According to the Hanafi School (as I understand it) performing *khilal/takhlil* (washing/rubbing between the toes or fingers) is performed **after** one washes the feet or hands because it is something done to compensate for any shortcomings in the obligatory aspects. This is evinced in the following manuals of Hanafi *fiqh*:

[1] "**(and)** rubbing between **(the fingers)** of the hand by interlacing them as well as the feet by the little finger of the left hand between the toes of his right foot. This is done after the water has reached between the toes..."[275]

(و) تخليل (الأصابع) اليدين بالتشبيك والرجلين بخنصر يده اليسرى بادئا بخنصر رجله اليمنى وهذا بعد دخول الماء خلالها...

[2] "...and doing *khilal* of the fingers before water has reached between the spaces of the fingers is a *fard* and after it is a *sunna*..."[276]

وتخليل الأصابع قبل وصول الماء إلى ما بين الأصابع فرض وبعده سنة...

---

[274] See al-Haskafi, *Durr al-Mukhtar*, 1:148.
[275] Ibn `Abidin, *Radd al-Muhtar*, 1:117.
[276] Ibn `Ala' al-Din, *al-Fatawa al-Tatarkhaniyya*, 1:94.

[3] "...doing *khilal* after washing three times because it one of the *sunna* that is performed three times..."[277]

وفي الظهيرية والتخليل إنما يكون بعد التثليث لأنه سنة التثليث...

[4] "...doing *takhlil* of the fingers and toes after water has reached between the spaces..."[278]

والثاني عشر تخليل الأصابع في اليدين والرجلين بعد إيصال الماء إلى ما بين الأصابع...

[5] "And this includes *takhlil* of the fingers [and toes] after water has reached between he spaces... *takhlil* is related to completing and perfecting the duty so it is a *sunna*..."[279]

ومنها تخليل الأصابع بعد إيصال الماء إلى منابتها...لإن التخليل من باب إكمال الفريضة فكان مسنونا...

[6] "and water reaching the tip of the fingers as well as between them is a *fard* whereas *takhlil* of the fingers after water has reached them is a *sunna*..."[280]

وإيصال الماء إلى رؤوس الأصابع وبين الأصابع فرض وتخليل الأصابع بعد إيصال الماء سنة...

[7] "[...] Shaykh Kamal al-Din Ibn al-Humam said that performing *takhlil* after [washing] is *mustahabb* mm"[281]

والوعيد في هذه الأحاديث [أي أحاديث تخليل الأصابع] محمول على إيصال الماء إلى ما بينها فإنه لا يجوز ترك ما خفي مما

[277] Ibn Nujaym, *al-Bahr al-Ra'iq*, 1:22.
[278] al-Samarqandi, *Tuhfat al-Fuqaha'*, 1:13.
[279] al-Kasani, *al-Bada'i` al-Sana'i`*, 1:114.
[280] al-Bukhari, *Khulasat al-Fatawa*, 1:22.
[281] al-Halabi, *Ghunyat al-Mutamalli*, p.24.

هو بينها كما يجوز في داخل اللحية

الكثيفة قال الشيخ كمال الدين بن الهمام

والتخليل بعد هذا مستحب لعدم المواظبة

مع كونه إكمالا في المحل.

[8] "And if water does not completely reach between the spaces of the fingers [and toes] then one must do *takhlil* three times after washing as mentioned in *al-Kifaya*..."[282]

وإن كانت الأصابع بحيث لا يصل الماء

فيما بينها يفرض تخليلها. ووقته بعد الغسل

ثلاثا كذا في الكفاية...

And Allah knows best.

19] Hair Removal Products

Q. Using hair removal products for armpits.

A.

There is nothing wrong in using contemporary hair removal products in order to remove:

1. hair on one's armpit;
2. hair on one's private parts (pubic hair) and
3. hair on one's body.[283]

---

[282] al-Ghunaymi, *Nihayat al-Murad*, p.110.
[283] Ibn `Abidin, *Radd al-Muhtar*, 6:407:

There is also nothing wrong with shaving these areas. These products are merely means to achieve an action. One can use other methods such as scissors clips, tweezers, etc. should it be desired:

"[...] it is permitted to shave the armpits although using tweezers is more preferable..."[284]

وفي الابط يجوز الحلق والنتف اولي ...

And Allah knows best.

20] Arousal and *Ghusl*

Q. I chat to gals and get aroused afterwards, do i have to do ghusl?

A.

Speaking to the opposite sex in and of itself does not constitute grounds for performing the full ritual bath (*ghusl*) although Islamic guidelines must be observed when conducting one's self around *ghayr mahram* females. As a basic rule the *fuqaha'* (Islamic legal scholars) give the following framework with regards to discharge of bodily fluid:

"[...] and in shaving of body hair and hair on the back there is lack of etiquette as mentioned in *al-Qunya*... and there is nothing wrong in shaving chest hair and back hair..."

وفي حلق شعر الصدر والظهر ترك الأدب كذا في القنية... ولا بأس في حلق شعر الصدر والظهر.

[284] See *al-Fatawa al-Hindiyya*, 5:358.

1. If semen (Ar. = *mani*) is discharged say through full ejaculation then this **will** necessitate the full purificatory bath (*ghusl*).

2. If pre-ejaculatory fluid (Ar. = *madhi*) is discharged say through erection and arousal then this **will not** necessitate the full purificatory bath.

3. If a clear liquid that precedes urine (Ar. = *wadi*) is released then this too **will not** necessitate the full purificatory bath.

So, only 1 (emission of semen) will require the full bath and 2 & 3 will only necessitate *wudu'*. If 2 and 3 is emitted and there is a noticeable residue (approximately 3cm in diameter) on the clothes, then unless that specific area is washed, *salah* will be considered *makruh* (disliked) but will nevertheless remain valid:

"(**emission of sperm**) which is a whitish fluid that softens up the penis up on its release and has a strong smell [...] and the scholars are all agreed that it is not necessary for a person to perform *ghusl* if they release *madhi* and *wadi*..."[285]

"...these are what require a bath [...] the emission of semen whether awake or asleep [...] and performing *ghusl* after releasing *madhi* and *wadi* is not obligatory."[286]

(خروج المني) وهو ماء أبيض ثخين ينكسر الذكر بخروجه يشبه رائحة الطلع. أجمع العلماء على أنه لا يجب الغسل بخروج المذي والودي.

وهذه النواقض للغسل ... إنزال المني فىى اليقظة أو في النوم...

ولا يجب الغسل من خروج مذي وودي.

[285] al-Tahtawi, *Hashiya `ala Maraqia al-Falah*, pp.96 and 101.
[286] al-Nabulusi, *Nihayat al-Murad*, pp.190 and 194.

And Allah knows best.

21] Dogs and Impurity

Q. Salam * does dog touchging [*sic.*] our clothes make it impure?**

A.

A number of things need to be mentioned regarding dogs, impurity (*najasa*) and requirements of cleanliness.

1. According to the dominant and most correct Hanafi view as stated by Imam Ahmad Reza Khan (Allah have mercy on him),[287] a dog is not impure in and of itself[288] only its saliva, blood and meat is. This was the opinion of Imam al-A`zam Abu Hanifa (ra) and it is the one taken in the school. Thus, if a dry dog say merely passes by brushing one's trousers then provided the dog did not pass on any impurities (faeces, etc) from the street, one will not need to wash the clothes and praying with the trousers will be valid:

"His saying (**a dog is not filthy of itself**) rather its meat and blood is impure [...].[289]	قوله (ليس الكلب بنجس العين) بل نجاسته بنجاسة لحمه ودمه ولا يظهر حكمها

وهي حي ما دامت في معدتها كنجاسة باطن

المصلي فهو كغيره من الحيوانات...

---

[287] See his fantastic discussion in *Salb al-Thalb `an Qa'ilin bi-Taharat al-Kalb* reproduced in his splendid *magnum opus* the *al-Fatawa al-Ridwiyya*, 4:399-472.

[288] Ibn `Abidin, *Radd al-Muhtar*, 1:139.

[289] Ibn `Abidin, *Radd al-Muhtar*, 1:207.

2. According to a lesser Hanafi opinion, if a wet dog shakes itself and the water falls on a person's clothes then it will render the affected areas of the clothes impure and hence it will require washing:

[...] إذا خرج الكلب من الماء وانتفض فأصاب ثوب إنسان أفسده لا لو أصابه ماء المطر لأن المبتل في الأول جلده وهو نجس وفي الثاني شعره وهو طاهر...

"[...] if a dog comes out of the water and shakes itself and then touches the clothes of a person, then it will be impure not if the rain water touches it because the decisive point in the first case is its skin (*jilduhu*)* which is impure whereas in the second case it is its hair which is pure..."[290]

*The view of Imam Ahmad Reza Khan is that the skin of a dog is not impure (*najas*) because if a dog is not unclean in its essence then this includes all its parts. He quotes from numerous Hanafi *fiqh* manuals one being Shaykh Zadeh's *Majma' al-Anhur*:

و اختلف في جلد الكلب والصحيح انه يطهر...

"[...] and some of [our jurists] differed over whether the hide/skin of dogs is pure or not; however the most correct opinion is that it is pure..."[291]

- Another opinion is that of Imam `Abd al-Hayy al-Laknawi's *al-Si`aya*:

يطهر الجلد الكلب أيضا بناء على ما عليه

"The skin of a dog too is pure based on the *fatwa* of the

[290] Ibn `Abidin, *Radd al-Muhtar*, 1:208.
[291] Shaykh Zadeh, *Majma' al-Anhur*, 1:32.

school declaring [the animal as] pure even though some of [our jurists] considered it impure..."[292]

الفتوى من طهارة عليه و ان رجح بعضهم

النجاسة...

3. If a dog playfully licks or bites onto an area of one's clothes, the affected area will have to be washed but if it bites out of anger gnashing with its teeth on the clothes then it will not require washing. The point to note is the moisture from the dog's saliva. If there is any contact with the saliva, the affected area will have to be washed because the dog's saliva is considered impure (*najis*):

"His saying (**and neither its bite**) meaning the bite of a dog onto one's clothes and his saying (**as long as no saliva is seen**) gives consideration to actually seeing any moisture or wetness which is the preferred view. And in *Nahr* of al-Sayrafiyya it has: what makes saliva evident is the moisture when one touches it. It is said that if a dog bites out of play and desire, it makes [the clothes] impure because moisture comes out of its lips which does not occur when it is angry because it bites down with its teeth..."[293]

قوله (ولا بعضه) أي عض الكلب الثوب

قوله (ما لم ير ريقه) فالمعتبر رؤية البلة

وهو المختار نهرعن الصيرفية وعلامتها

ابتلال يده بأخذه وقيل لو عض في الرضا

نجسه لأنه يأخذ بشفته الرطبة لا في

الغضب لأخذه بأسنانه...

And Allah knows best.

---

[292] al-Laknawi, *al-Si'aya fi Kashf ma fi Sharh al-Wiqaya*, 1:409.
[293] Ibn 'Abidin, *Radd al-Muhtar*, 1:208.

22] *Wudu'* and Boxer Shorts

Q. wudu in boxer shorts.

A.

Doing *wudu'* with just boxer shorts on does not invalidate it (neither does being naked). However, Islamic dress requirements stipulate one **must** cover at least from his navel to his knees in the presence of others otherwise it will be a sin:

**"(the `*awra* of a man is from under his navel to his knees)** based on the saying of the Messenger of Allah: 'the `*awra* of a man is from his navel to his knees'..."[294]

...(وعورة الرجل ما تحت السرة إلى الركبة) لقوله عليه الصلاة والسلام {عورة الرجل ما بين سرته إلى ركبته }...

And Allah knows best.

23] Breaking *Wudu'* while performing *Wudu'*

Q. Breaking wind when doing wudu.

A.

If one passes wind while performing *wudu'*, then one must repeat it. The conditions that nullify *wudu'* enter into effect when commencing it.

And Allah knows best.

---

[294] al-Marghinani, *al-Hidaya*, 1:92.

24] Wiping the Head with Gel on it

Q. I was speaking to some brothers and they told me that i cant wipe over my head if i have gel on. When im at work i put gel on and it means washing my hair everytime i pray that will become impractical for me. Does this count as necessity or is there some kind of Islamic evidence to say i can just wipe over. jzk

A.

Firstly, there are different types of gel or hair styling products. Some are thick and do leave the hair strong and extra firm stiffening the locks into a hold while others have thinner substance that shape and hold the hair but have no lasting strong residue.

Secondly, the general condition for *wudu'* in our school is that water must reach the skin when washing so if a barrier exists then until that barrier is removed, the *wudu'* will not be valid:

"And his statement (**the same applies if he applies any oil**) like oil or lubricants and sesame oil different from grease or solid fat. His statement (*al-dasuma* [S. a type of fatty grease]) is the remains of the oil as mentioned by al-Shurunbulali. al-Maqdisi said: In *al-Fatawa* it mentions, 'he applied oil to his feet and then performed *wudu'* and [thereafter] poured [water] across his legs and water did not reach [the required area] due to the oil'.

قوله " و كذا دهن" اى كزيت و شيرج بخلاف نحو شحم و سمن جامد "قوله و دسومة" هى اثر الدهن قال فى الشرنبلالية قال المقدسى : و فى الفتاوى دهن رجليه ثم توضأ و امرّ على رجليه و لم يقبل الماء للدسومة جاز لوجود غسل الرجلين...

This is permitted due to the feet being washed..."[295]

"My father, may Allah Most High have mercy on him, said that if one applies oil to his feet and then pours water and it does not reach [the skin] due to the oily area, wudu' is still permitted as mentioned in Khazanat al-Fatawa. In Majmu' al-Nawazil it has: washing requires pouring water over the parts without it sticking. If he oils those parts of the body required for wudu' and then pours water over them and it does not stick to the skin, then it is permitted."[296]

قال والدى رحمه الله تعالى اذا دهن رجليه

و امرّ الماء و لم يصل لمكان الدسومات

, جاز الوضوء كما فى " خزانة الفتاوى "

و فى "مجموع النوازل" : الغسل يقتضى

جواز اسالة الماء على الاعضاء دون

الازاق فلو دهن اعضاء الوضوء ثم سال

عليها الملء و لم يلتزق عليها جاز .

Thirdly, you may need to check the kind of gel product you are using. If it is thin like gum, wax or oil then there usually is no strong barrier created around the hair and wiping over the head will be valid and no washing of the hair prior to wudu' will be necessary. If however the product you are using is not thin like the aforementioned ones, then you may need to change your hair product because there will be no shar'i (legal) exemption as it is not a case for it and neither is it a case of necessity (darura) as no necessity exists to apply hair gel as one can do without it.

Therefore, the general advice given to you by this brother does not hold. You may perform the wipe (mash) over the head with an appropriate hair gel.

---

[295] Ibn 'Abidin, Radd al-Muhtar, 1:154.
[296] al-Ghunaymi, Nihayat al-Murad, p.81.

And Allah knows best.

25] Shortening the *wudu'* for fear of missing the Prayer

Q. I heard that if one fears missing the salah in the mosque, one can shorten the wudu and join the prayer. Is this correct?

A.

If one is sure that one will miss the congregation prayer (*salat al-jama`a*) by performing the full *wudu'*, then one may contract it (meaning doing the obligatory aspects [s: washing the face, washing the hands, washing the feet and wiping a quarter of the head]) and join the *salah*. This is mentioned from a related ruling in the Hanafi manual of Imam Ibn `Abidin regarding contraction of (shortening) the *sunna* prayer:

"If one fears that by praying the *sunna* of Fajr prayer and because of it the congregational prayer will elapse and one then shortens the prayer by reciting the Fatiha chapter along with the supplications in both bowing (*ruku`*) and prostration (*sujud*) then he may do that because leaving the performance of a *sunna* is permitted (*ja'iz*) if it means catching the congregational prayer..."[297]	لو خاف انّه لو صلى سنة الفجر بوجهها تفوته الجماعة و لو اقتصر فيها بالفاتحة و تسبحة فى الركوع و السجود يدركها فله ان يقتصر عليها لانّ ترك السنة جائز لادراك الجماعة...

---

[297] Ibn `Abidin, *Radd al-Muhtar*, 2:58.

If however, one is sure that the congregational prayer **will not** be missed, then there arise three scenarios with their respective rulings:

Scenario one: If one completes the full *wudu'* and the first *takbir* (s: saying 'Allahu Akbar!' when commencing the *salah*) is missed but despite that the first *rak`a* is caught, then in this case a full *wudu'* should be performed:

"If one thinks that one will miss the first and commencing *takbir* (al-takbirat al-ula) then one must perform the *wudu'* completely [s: literally '*tathlith*' - washing the limbs three times which is a *sunna*]. If the *takbirat al-ula* elapses but the congregational prayer did not finish completely such that if he is able to catch one *rak`a* with the imam standing or by doing the *ruku`* then it is better (*afdal*) to complete the *wudu'* than to catch the *takbirat al-ula* because catching the *takbirat al-ula* with the Imam is an additional virtue and not a *sunna*...*"*[298]

ان ظنّ انّه تفوته التكبيرة الاولى فالتثليث

افضل. و اذا فاتته التبيرة الاولى فقط

لم تفته الصلاة بالجماعة اجماعا حتى

لو كان يدرك الامام راكعا و يحصل معه

الركوع حيث لا تفوته الركعة فاتيانه يسنّة

التثليث افضل من ادراكه اوّل الركعة لانّ

ادراك التكبيرة مع الامام فضيلة لا

سنّة...

Scenario two: If one begins *wudu'* at such a time where if the full *wudu'* is performed the first *rak`a* of the *salah* will be missed but doing a contracted *wudu'* will mean catching the first *rak`a* then in this case it is preferable to perform a contracted *wudu'* and catch the first *rak`a*:

---

[298] al-Ghunaymi, *Nihayat al-Murad*, p.114.

"[...] if one thinks that doing the full *wudu'* [s: literally '*tathlith*' - washing the limbs three times which is a *sunna*] will mean missing a *rak`a* of the *salah* with the congregation then he may contract the *wudu'*..."[299]

ان ظنّ انّه ان ثلث الوضوء تفوته ركعة من الصلاة مع الجماعة يترك التثليث...

Scenario three: If *wudu'* is commenced at such a time wherein the first *rak`a* has already finished and one is sure that by doing a full *wudu'* no part of the congregation *salah* will be missed, then in this case it would be better to perform the complete *wudu'*:

"[...] if for example one caught a single *rak`a* of the Zuhr prayer then he has attained the excellence (*fadl*) of the congregation or its reward. Likewise, if one catches the *Tashahhud* then he has attained its excellence according to their view because the point here is attaining the excellence and reward of the congregation and in their agreement that by catching the Tashahhud he has attained [the Prayer], he has also thereby accomplished the *sunna*..."[300]

انّ من ادرك ركعة من الظهر مثلا فقد ادرك فضل الجماعة و احرز ثوابها و كذا لو ادرك التشهد يكون مدركا لفضيلتها على قولهم لانّ المدار هنا على ادراك فضل الجماعة و قد اتّفقوا على ادراكه بادراك التشهد فيأتى بالسنّة اتّفاقا...

And Allah knows best.

---

[299] al-Ghunaymi, *Nihayat al-Murad*, p.114.
[300] Ibn `Abidin, *Radd al-Muhtar*, 3:56.

26] Mud on Clothes

Q. A little mud on clothes.

A.

There is no harm if a little splatter of mud or traces of mud appear on one's clothes and h/she then prays. This is overlooked. However, if able to, it is better to wipe or wash away the mud traces.

"As for a little impurity (*al-najasa al-qalila*), it does not make prayer impermissible regardless of whether it is light (*khafifa*) or heavy (*ghaliza*) based on istihsan..."[301]

أما النجاسة القليلة فإنها لا تمنع جواز الصلاة، سواء كانت خفيفة أو غليظة استحسانا...

And Allah knows best.

27] Permissibility of having a Jacuzzi

Q. Is having a Jacuzzi haram?

A.

No. Having a Jacuzzi in one's house is not unlawful.

And Allah knows best.

---

[301] See al-Kasani, *Bada'i` al-Sana'i`*, 1:232.

28] *Wudu'* with running water

Q. what about wudhu under a running tap. Many people just wash their body parts but not three times. Is this wudhu valiod [*sic.*]?

A.

The *wudu'* will be valid. However, it is *sunna* to wash the required body parts three times and one may **NOT** perform *wudu'* by habitually leaving this *sunna*. In Imam al-Zayla`i's commentary of Imam al-Nasafi's *Kanz al-Daqa'iq* it states regarding the *sunna* aspects of *wudu'*:

"...(and washing three times) because [the Prophet] – upon him be blessings and peace – performed *wudu'* washing three times saying 'this is my *wudu'* and that of the Prophets before me'..."[302]	...(وَتَثْلِيثُ الْغَسْلِ) لِأَنَّهُ صلى الله عليه وسلم تَوَضَّأَ ثَلَاثًا ثَلَاثًا وقال هذا وُضُوئِي وَوُضُوءُ الْأَنْبِيَاءِ من قَبْلِي...

And Allah knows best.

29] Touching Private Parts and *Wudu'*

Q. does touching private parts make me do wudoo again?

A.

No. This is a point of difference amongst our noble *fuqaha'* across schools.

---

[302] See al-Zayla`i, *Tabyin al-Haqa'iq Sharh Kanz al-Daqa'iq*, 1:4. Bracketed text in bold is that of Imam al-Nasafi's text *Kanz al-Daqa'iq*.

However, in the *madhhab* of the Imam al-A`zam Abu Hanifa (Allah be pleased with him), after performing *wudu'* ('ritual ablution') if one accidentally or intentionally touches his private parts, then the *wudu'* does not have to be repeated. Imam al-Zayla`i writes:

"...(and touching the private parts) i.e. touching it does not invalidate the *wudu'* and it is connected to the previous things that do not invalidate the *wudu'* and this is the opinion of `Umar ibn al-Khattab, `Ali b. Abi Talib, Ibn Mas`ud, Ibn `Abbas, Zayd b. Thabit and others from the senior *Sahaba* and *Tabi'un* (successors) such as al-Hasan al-Basri, Sa`id b. al-Musayyib and al-Thawri. [Imam] al-Tahawi said: we do not know anyone of the *Sahaba* who issued this kind of *fatwa* for *wudu'* except Ibn `Umar but the majority opposed him in that..."[303]

(وَمَسُّ ذَكَرٍ) أَيْ مَسُّهُ لَا يَنْقُضُ الْوُضُوءَ وهو مَعْطُوفٌ على غَيْرِ النَّاقِضِ وهو مَذْهَبُ عُمَرَ بن الْخَطَّابِ وَعَلِيٍّ بن أبي طَالِبٍ وَابْنِ مَسْعُودٍ وَابْنِ عَبَّاسٍ وَزَيْدِ بن ثَابِتٍ وَغَيْرِهِمْ من كِبَارِ الصَّحَابَةِ وَصُدُورِ التَّابِعِينَ مِثْلُ الْحَسَنِ الْبَصْرِيِّ وَسَعِيدِ بن الْمُسَيِّبِ وَالثَّوْرِيِّ وقال الطَّحَاوِيُّ لم نَعْلَمْ أَحَدًا من الصَّحَابَةِ أَفْتَى بِالْوُضُوءِ منه غير ابْنِ عُمَرَ وقد خَالَفَهُ أَكْثَرُهُمْ...

And Allah knows best.

---

[303] See al-Zayla`i, *Tabyin al-Haqa'iq*, 1:11. The text in bracket and bold is that of Imam al-Nasafi's *Kanz al-Daqa'iq*.

30] Praying with the urge to relieve

Q. Praying but holding myself from breaking wind. Is this allowed?

A.

If your worry is that the *salah* will be invalidated then unless you actually break wind, the *wudu'* will remain. The condition that invalidates the *wudu'* is any actual emission of fluid (semen, urine, blood, etc.) or release (wind, gas, etc.).

And Allah knows best.

31] *Ghusl* and washing private parts properly

Q. I didn't wash myself properly while going to the toilet does that mean i have to do the ghusl?

A.

It will suffice to wash the private areas and change your clothes. This would enable you to perform *salah* as normal. No *ghusl* will be required.

And Allah knows best.

32] *Wudu'* and contact lenses

Q. We play football and use contacts. Do i have to take them off when i do wudhu. I was told that i have to but that would make things difficult.

A.

For *wudu'*, the requirement is to wash the external areas of the face (which is considered to the beginning part of the forehead to the bottom of the chin).[304] The eye and eyeball is considered as the internal part of the face and so would not require to be washed and therefore the contact lenses would not have to be removed. Your *wudu'* will be valid and hence your *salah* will be valid too.

And Allah knows best.

33] Breaking wind and *Ghusl*

Q. salam bro does breaking wind invalidate the ghusl?

A.

Breaking wind during the full ritual bath (*ghusl*) does not invalidate it; however *wudu'* is invalidated. Imam al-Quduri writes in his primer on *fiqh* about that which obligates *ghusl*:

And those aspects that necessitate *ghusl* are: [1] the emission of semen by way of spurting or excitement in a man and woman; [2] Contact of the two circumcised parts [even] without emission; [3] menstruation and [4] post-natal bleeding..."[305]	والمعاني الموجبة للغسل : إنزال المني على وجه الدفق والشهوة من الرجل والمرأة والتقاء الختانين من غير إنزال والحيض والنفاس

Imam al-Shurunbulali in his primer on Hanafi *fiqh* on the devotional 5 pillars of Islam writes:

---

[304] See al-Ghunaymi, *al-Lubab fi Sharh al-Kitab*, 1:31.
[305] al-Quduri, *al-Mukhtasar*, p.40.

"12 things invalidate *wudu'*: [1] whatever exits the two passageways except air from the rear according to the most correct opinion [...]."[306]

ينقض الوضوء اثنا عشرة شيئا ما خرج من السبيلين إلا ريح القبل في الأصح ...

And Allah knows best.

34] Praying on urinated Floor

Q. My baby boy urinated on the floor and later i prayed over that area not knowing. Is my prayer valid?

A.

If the area of the floor or ground the urine fell on dried up such that it was no longer visible or noticeable (in either colour or smell) and a prayer mat was placed over it and *salah* was offered it would be valid. This will not be considered an instance where filth remains or transfers. Imam al-Marghinani states:

"**(If filth falls on the ground and the sun dries it up and the traces disappear, prayer over that spot will be permitted)**. Zufar and al-Shafi`i (Allah have mercy on both) however did not permit it because no purifying factor (*al-muzil*) is present **(and)** therefore **(performing *tayammum* would not be permitted with it)**. We have the statement of the Prophet

(وَإِنْ أَصَابَتِ الْأَرْضَ نَجَاسَةٌ فَجَفَّتْ بِالشَّمْسِ وَذَهَبَ أَثَرُهَا جَازَتْ الصَّلَاةُ عَلَى مَكَانِهَا) وَقَالَ زُفَرُ وَالشَّافِعِيُّ رَحِمَهُمَا اللَّهُ لَا تَجُوزُ لِأَنَّهُ لَمْ يُوجَدْ الْمُزِيلُ (وَ) لِهَذَا (لَا يَجُوزُ التَّيَمُّمُ بِهِ) وَلَنَا قَوْلُهُ عَلَيْهِ الصَّلَاةُ وَالسَّلَامُ { ذَكَاةُ الْأَرْضِ يُبْسُهَا } وَإِنَّمَا لَا

---

[306] al-Surunbulali, *Nur al-Idah*, p.35.

(upon him be blessings and peace): "land is purified when it dries up"...."[307]

يَجُوزُ التَّيَمُّمُ بِهِ لِأَنَّ طَهَارَةَ الصَّعِيدِ ثَبَتَتْ شَرْطًا بِنَصِّ الْكِتَابِ فَلَا تَتَأَدَّى بِمَا ثَبَتَ بِالْحَدِيثِ

- Imam al-Zayla`i writes:

"al-Marghinani[308] mentioned that if an object is dry but pure it can become impure due to it coming into contact with the wetness of a damp but impure substance. If the dry object is something impure and [comes into contact with] something damp but pure then the latter will not become impure because the impure object acquires the dampness from the pure damp substance and the damp substance does not acquire anything whatsoever from the dry object – and what he means by that is when the thing separates onto the damp substance. His words indicate this in where he mentions dampness being transferred. Therefore, on the meaning we just mentioned, if a wet cloth was spread over a dry but impure item, then the cloth will not become impure. Al-

وذكر المرغيناني إن كان اليابس هو الطاهر يتنجس لأنه يأخذ بللا من النجس الرطب، وإن كان اليابس هو النجس والطاهر الرطب لا يتنجس لأن اليابس النجس يأخذ بللا من الطاهر، ولا يأخذ الرطب من اليابس شيئا، ويحمل على أن مراده فيما إذا كان الرطب ينفصل منه شيء، وفي لفظه إشارة إليه حيث نص على أخذ البلة، وعلى هذا إذا نشر الثوب المبلول على حبل نجس، وهو يابس لا يتنجس الثوب لما ذكرنا من المعنى، وقال قاضيخان في فتاواه إذا نام الرجل على فراش فأصابه مني ويبس وعرق الرجل،

---

[307] al-Marghinani, *al-Hidaya* in *Fath al-Qadir* of Imam Ibn al-Humam, 1:366-388.
[308] See *al-Hidaya* (English translation), 1:70-71.

Qadikhan in his *fatawa* mentions that if a man sleeps on his bed and emitted semen and it dried and he then sweated such that the bed was wet due to his sweat, then if the effects of any wetness are not apparent on his body then it is not rendered impure. If the sweat was a lot such that the bed was really wet and then the wetness of the bed affected his body and the effect was apparent, his body would become impure. The same holds for if a person washes his feet and walks over an impure part of the ground and the ground was made wet and dark from the water of his feet but no wetness from the ground could be seen on his feet and he then prayed, his prayer will be valid. If however, the wetness of the water from his feet was a lot such that the ground was covered in wetness because of it and formed a kind of mud (or mixture) and this caught to his feet then his prayer will not be valid. If he was to walk on wet ground that is impure and his feet are dry, it will become impure...”[309]

وابتل الفراش من عرقه إن لم يظهر له أثر البلل في بدنه لا يتنجس جسده، وإن كان العرق كثيرا حتى ابتل الفراش ثم أصاب بلل الفراش جسده، وظهر أثره في جسده يتنجس بدنه، وكذا الرجل إذا غسل رجله فمشى على أرض نجسة بغير مكعب فابتل الأرض من بلل رجله، واسود وجه الأرض لكن لم يظهر أثر بلل الأرض في رجله فصلى جازت صلاته، وإن كان بلل الماء في رجله كثيرا حتى ابتل به وجه الأرض، وصار طينا ثم أصاب الطين رجله لا تجوز صلاته، ولو مشى على أرض نجسة رطبة، ورجله يابسة تتنجس.

---

[309] See al-Zayla`i, *Tabyin al-Haqa'iq Sharh Kanz al-Daqa'iq*, 18:327.

And Allah knows best.

35] Using Washing Machines to Purify Ckothes

Q. Is washing clothes in a washing machine permitted?

A.

Yes.

"...however, what is in the *Sharh al-Munya* follows what is in *al-Muhit*. He then said: the point being that the traces [of the impurity] have to be removed in all places as much as possible without hardship with whatever one can to ensure this. The *Hashiya* of al-Wani of *al-Durar* has something similar where he (Allah have mercy on him) said: I say: I know that what is considered in purifying visible impurities is removal of the impurity itself[310] even with one wash or within an *ijjana*[311] as was mentioned. Neither washing three times nor duration itself is a condition. As for non-visible impurities, what is considered is either one's strongest guess as to the purification without necessarily

لكن في شرح المنية تعقب ما في المحيط ثم قال : فالحاصل أن زوال الأثر شرط في كل موضع ما لم يشق كيفما كان التطهير وبأي شيء كان فليحفظ ذلك ١ هـ ونحوه في حاشية الواني على الدرر و قال (رحمه الله تعالى) : أقول : لكن قد علمت أن المعتبر في تطهير النجاسة المرئية زوال عينها ولو بغسلة واحدة ولو في إجانة كما مر، فلا يشترط فيها تثليث غسل ولا عصر، وأن المعتبر غلبة الظن في تطهير غير المرئية بلا عدد على المفتى به أو

---

[310] Or the impure substance.

[311] A kind of trough or a single concave container like a basin that has an open top which is filled with water.

the number [of washes] – and according to this understanding the *fatwa* is given – or with the condition of washing three times as was mentioned earlier. No doubt, washing with running water and whatever falls under its ruling such as a stream or pouring a lot of water which fundamentally removes the impurity and anything else that substitutes repeated flow of water is stronger than washing in an [instrument such as] an *ijjana* which opposes *qiyas*. This is because the impurity in it mixes with the water and circulates in all parts of the clothes and equating both methods regarding the condition of three washes is farfetched. Its condition is not a ruling that is devotional (*ta'abbudiyan*) such that it is binding even if the meaning is not understood. So for that reason, Imam al-Halwani says based on an analogy with the statement of Abu Yusuf regarding the cloth for the baths that: if the impurity is blood or urine and water is poured over it, it will suffice and what is mentioned in *al-Fath* [*al-Qadir*] is that this was out of necessity for covering the `awra. The response in *al-Bahr* [*al-Ra'iq*] as taken from

مع شرط التثليث على ما مر ولا شك أن الغسل بالماء الجاري وما في حكمه من الغدير أو الصب الكثير الذي يذهب بالنجاسة أصلا ويخلفه غيره مرارا بالجريان أقوى من الغسل في الإجانة التي على خلاف القياس لأن النجاسة فيها تلاقي الماء وتسري معه في جميع أجزاء الثوب فيبعد كل البعد التسوية بينهما في اشتراط التثليث، وليس اشتراطه حكما تعبديا حتى يلتزم وإن لم يعقل معناه، ولهذا قال الإمام الحلواني على قياس قول أبي يوسف في إزار الحمام : إنه لو كانت النجاسة دما أو بولا وصب عليه الماء كفاه، وقول الفتح إن ذلك لضرورة ستر العورة كما مر رده في البحر بما في السراج، وأقره في النهر وغيره...

al-Siraj and *al-Nahr* [*al-Fa'iq*] as well as other books was discussed earlier..."[312]

And Allah knows best.

36] *Wudu'* and touching Qur'an translations

Q. whether wudu' is required to touch and read English Qur'an translations without the Arabic.

A.

In the Hanafi compendium of legal discussions and edicts *al-Fatawa al-Hindiyya* it states:

"If the Qur'an is written down in Persian it is disliked to touch it according to Abu Hanifa and the two [Imams Abu Yusuf and al-Shaybani] which is the most correct understanding. In *al-Khulasa* it has the same..."[313]

وَلَوْ كَان الْقُرْآنُ مَكْتُوبًا بِالْفَارِسِيَّةِ يُكْرَهُ لهم مَسُّهُ عِنْدَ أبي حَنِيفَةَ وَكَذَا عِنْدَهُمَا على الصَّحِيحِ هَكَذَا في الْخُلَاصَةِ...

Therefore, if the Qur'an translation is English or any other language, it ought not to be touched without the ritual ablution (*wudu'*).

And Allah knows best.

---

[312] See Ibn 'Abidin, *Radd al-Muhtar*, 1:222.
[313] See *al-Fatawa al-Hindiyya*, 1:38 and Mufti Abdul Wahid Qadiri, *Fatawa Europe*, p.102.

37] *Wudu'* and blood on the *miswak*

Q. I used a miswak and saw blood on it. Do i have to repeat wudu?

A.

- In the *al-Fatawa al-Hindiyya* it states the following:

"If a person with *wudu'* bites down on something and sees traces of blood on it or uses a *miswak* and sees traces of blood on it, his *wudu'* will not be invalidated as long as it does not flow. The same is mentioned in *al-Zahiriyya...*"[314]

المتوضي اذ غض شيأ فوجد فيه اثر الدم أو استاك بسواك فوجد فيه اثر الدم لم ينقض ما لم يعرف السيلان كذا في الظهيرية...

Thus, the mere visibility of blood does not necessarily invalidate the *wudu'* and so it will not have to be repeated.

Using the *Miswak* is a *sunna* and recommended[315] and hence fears of blood traces should not discourage one from using it.

And Allah knows best.

---

[314] See *al-Fatawa al-Hindiyya*, 1:11 and Mufti Abdul Wahid Qadiri, *Fatawa Europe*, p.117.
[315] See Mufti Abdul Wahid Qadiri, *Fatawa Europe*, pp.118-121 for elaboration.

38] *Wudu'* and Sleep

Q. When does wudu break sleeping?

A.

A few points need clarifying here. Contrary to misconceptions, sleeping itself is not something that invalidates *wudu*[316] but with other conditions can invalidate it, e.g. if a person sleeps such that h/her limbs are fully relaxed so there is no way of being certain whether gas was passed during that time.[317] If one sleeps in a position where the bottom or rear part is firmly pressed or rooted on the ground or any object/space (e.g. a sofa, chair, settee, platform, etc.) then the *wudu'* will not be invalidated but in any other position such as reclining on one's side or lying down straight will invalidate it. In *al-Muhit al-Burhani* of Mahmud al-Bukhari it has:

"If one sleeps in a sitting posture with his buttocks firmly on the ground, his *wudu'* will not be invalidated. If he sleeps while sitting on a level platform but leaning upon a wall or a pillar (*ustuwana*), then Shams al-A'imma al-Halwani (Allah have mercy on him) stated that the most predominant position (*zahir al-madhhab*) of the School is that it does not invalidate the *wudu'*..."[318]

إذا نام قاعداً مسوياً إليتيه على الأرض لا ينتقض وضوءه، وإن نام قاعداً (على) مستوى الجلوس، ولكن مستنداً إلى جدار أو أسطوانة، ذكر شمس الأئمة الحلواني رحمه الله أن ظاهر المذهب أنه لا ينتقض وضوءه.

---

[316] Mufti Abdul Wahid Qadiri, *Fatawa Europe*, p.140.
[317] Mufti Abdul Wahid Qadiri, *Fatawa Europe*, p.140.
[318] al-Bukhari, *al-Muhit al-Burhani*, 1, fol.7a.

And Allah knows best.

39] Tooth fillings and *Ghusl*

Q. Tooth Fillings and wudu/ghusl.

A.

Firstly, it is permitted to have tooth fillings especially if there is a need. Secondly, *wudu'* will be valid with fillings and they do not have to be removed as this would be in most cases extremely difficult to do.

"And Muhammad [ibn al-Hasan al-Shaybani] – may Allah Most High have mercy on him – said in *al-Jami` al-Saghir*: teeth should not be filled with gold although they may be with silver; meaning if [the teeth] wobble and there is a fear they will fall out so one fills it in with silver and not gold; this is also the opinion of Abu Hanifa – Allah most high have mercy on him. Muhammad – Allah most high have mercy on him – said: one may also fill his teeth with gold. The opinion of Abu Yusuf – Allah most high have mercy on him – was not mentioned in *al-Jami` al-Saghir*. It is said by some that his opinion accorded with Abu Hanifa – Allah most high have mercy on him. Al-Hakim

قَالَ مُحَمَّدٌ – رحمه الله تعالى – في الْجَامِعِ الصَّغِيرِ وَلَا يَشُدُّ الْأَسْنَانَ بِالذَّهَبِ وَيَشُدُّهَا بِالْفِضَّةِ يُرِيدُ بِه إذَا تَحَرَّكَتْ الْأَسْنَانُ وَخِيفَ سُقُوطُهَا فَأَرَادَ صَاحِبُهَا أَنْ يَشُدَّهَا يَشُدُّهَا بِالْفِضَّةِ وَلَا يَشُدُّهَا بِالذَّهَبِ وَهَذَا قَوْلُ أَبِي حَنِيفَةَ – رحمه الله تعالى – وَقَالَ مُحَمَّدٌ – رحمه الله تعالى – يَشُدُّهَا بِالذَّهَبِ أَيْضًا وَلَمْ يَذْكُرْ في الْجَامِعِ الصَّغِيرِ قَوْلَ أَبِي يُوسُفَ – رحمه الله تعالى – قِيلَ : هُوَ مَعَ مُحَمَّدٍ – رحمه الله تعالى – وَقِيلَ : هُوَ مَعَ أَبِي حَنِيفَةَ – رحمه الله تعالى – وَذَكَرَ الْحَاكِمُ في

mentions in *al-Multaqa*: if a man's teeth begins to wobble and he fears it will fall out and he fills it with gold or silver, then there is nothing wrong with this according to Abu Hanifa and Abu Yusuf – Allah most high have mercy on them both. And al-Hasan narrates from Abu Hanifa – Allah most high have mercy on him – that he made a differentiation between teeth and the nose. Regarding teeth, he said there is nothing wrong in them being filled with gold whereas with regards to the nose, it is disliked as mentioned in *al-Muhit* [al-Burhani]. Abu Yusuf – Allah most high have mercy on him – said: there is nothing wrong if a person attempts to pull out his own teeth or to fill it himself. However, it is disliked if [these are done to] another's teeth as mentioned in *al-Siraj al-Wahhaj*. A man reported saying: I asked Abu Hanifa – Allah most high have mercy on him – regarding this matter and he saw nothing wrong with it as mentioned in *al-Dhakhira*...”[319]

الْمُنْتَقَى لَوْ تَحَرَّكَتْ سِنُّ رَجُلٍ وَخَافَ سُقُوطَهَا فَشَدَّهَا بِالذَّهَبِ أَوْ بِالْفِضَّةِ لَمْ يَكُنْ بِهِ بَأْسٌ عِنْدَ أَبِي حَنِيفَةَ وَأَبِي يُوسُفَ – رَحِمَهُمَا اللَّهُ تَعَالَى – وَرَوَى الْحَسَنُ عَنْ أَبِي حَنِيفَةَ – رحمه الله تعالى – أَنَّهُ فَرَّقَ بَيْنَ السِّنِّ وَالْأَنْفِ فَقَالَ فِي السِّنِّ لَا بَأْسَ بِأَنْ يَشُدَّهَا بِالذَّهَبِ وَفِي الْأَنْفِ كُرِهَ ذَلِكَ كَذَا فِي الْمُحِيطِ . وَقَالَ أَبُو يُوسُفَ – رحمه الله تعالى – لَا بَأْسَ بِأَنْ يُعِيدَ سِنَّ نَفْسِهِ وَأَنْ يَشُدَّهَا وَإِنْ كَانَ سِنَّ غَيْرِهِ يُكْرَهُ ذَلِكَ كَذَا فِي السِّرَاجِ الْوَهَّاجِ . قَالَ بِشْرٌ قَالَ أَبُو يُوسُفَ – رحمه الله تعالى – فِي مَجْلِسٍ آخَرَ سَأَلْتُ أَبَا حَنِيفَةَ – رحمه الله تعالى – عَنْ ذَلِكَ فَلَمْ يَرَ بِإِعَادَتِهَا بَأْسًا كَذَا فِي الذَّخِيرَةِ...

---

[319] See *al-Fatawa al-Hindiyya*, 5:336. See also, al-Tahawi, *Sharh Ma`ani al-Athar*, 4:257; al-Kasani, *al-Bada`i` al-Sana`i`* 5:132 and Ibn `Abidin, *Radd al-Muhtar*, 5:231

Thirdly, the position of the Hanafi School in permitting tooth fillings is actually an indication of its acceptance and validity for ritual requirements, e.g. *wudu'* and *ghusl* and not an invalidator (*nawaqid*).

And Allah knows best.

40] Standing and urinating

Q. Salam *** brother asked is it permitted to stand and urinate? Ws

A.

In the Hanafi School, it is somewhat disliked to stand and urinate as discussed in Imam Ibn `Abidin's *Radd al-Muhtar*:

"His statement: (**and if he stands and urinates**) due to the discouragement of doing it based on the statement of `A'isha (ra) that the Prophet (saw) only urinated in a sitting posture as narrated by Ahmad, al-Tirmidhi and al-Nasa'i and its *isnad* is good (*jayyid*). Imam al-Nawawi states in his commentary on the *Sahih* of Muslim: the *hadith*s that have been transmitted regarding the prohibition [s: of urinating while standing] are not established. However, the *hadith* of `A'isha is established and for that reason the scholars	قوله: (وأن يبول قائما) لما ورد من النهي عنه، ولقول عائشة رضي الله عنها: من حدثكم أن النبي (صلى الله عليه و سلم) كان يبول قائما فلا تصدقوه، ما كان يبول إلا قاعدا رواه أحمد والترمذي والنسائي وإسناده جيد. قال النووي في شرح مسلم: وقد روي في النهي أحاديث لا تثبت، ولكن حديث عائشة ثابت فلذا قال العلماء: يكره إلا لعذر،

have said that it is disliked [s: to stand and urinate] unless one has a genuine excuse [s: such as an injury to the back, posture trouble, non-availability of a toilet, etc.]. The dislike is slight but not prohibitive..."[320]

وهي كراهة تنزيه لا تحريم.

And Allah knows best.

41] Baby vomit and impurity

Q. Baby vomit and cleaning clothes

A.

Baby vomit (whether with or without solids) is considered impure (*najis*). If a baby vomit lands on a surface or area, it should be washed three times or until it is removed. If it lands on your clothes, then the affected area should be washed and rinsed and then squeezed at each wash until the vomit traces are removed.

"As for the different types of impurities (*al-anjas*) one of them is what al-Karkhi mentioned in his *Mukhtasar*: anything that exits from the human body due to which *wudu'* and *ghusl* is necessitated, then this is considered as an impurity (*najis*) such as: urine, excrement, *wadi*, *madhi* (pre-coital fluid), *mani* (semen),

أما أنواع الأنجاس فمنها ما ذكره الكرخي في مختصره أن كل ما يخرج من بدن الإنسان مما يجب بخروجه الوضوء أو الغسل فهو نجس من البول والغائط والودي والمذي والمني ودم الحيض والنفاس والاستحاضة والدم السائل من الجرح والصديد والقيء ملء الفم

وأما شرائط التطهير بالماء فمنها العدد في

[320] Ibn 'Abidin, *Radd al-Muhtar*, 1:344.

blood, menses, pre-natal fluid (al-nifas), bleeding (al-istihada), flowing blood from a wound, pus and a mouthful of vomit...[321]

As for one of the conditions for purifying with water, then according to our position it is to wash the impurity repeatedly if it is not-visible. In general, impurities are of two types: actual (haqiqiyya) and ritual (hukmiyya). There is no difference over [the types] of ritual impurities such as minor ritual impurity (hadath), major ritual impurity (janaba) which are removed by a single wash and it is not a condition that one repeatedly wash. As for actual ritual impurity, if it is not visible like urine and things like that, then the authentically transmitted position of the school (zahir al-riwaya) is purification is achived by washing three times..."[322]

And Allah knows best.

نجاسة غير مرئية عندنا والجملة في ذلك أن النجاسة نوعان حقيقية وحكمية ولا خلاف في أن النجاسة الحكمية وهي الحدث والجنابة تزول بالغسل مرة واحدة ولا يشترط فيها العدد وأما النجاسة الحقيقية فإن كانت غير مرئية كالبول ونحوه ذكر في ظاهر الرواية أنه لا تطهر إلا بالغسل ثلاثا...

---

[321] al-Kasani, al-Bada'i` al-Sana'i`, 1:193.
[322] al-Kasani, al-Bada'i` al-Sana'i`, 1:248.

42] Making Supplications while in the Shower

Q. *Du`a'* while in the shower.

A.

Normally, a bathroom is not a place of supplication, i.e. a location where one makes the intention to visit and perform intentional pleas and supplications and neither is it a place where the required mood of reverence and humility for that is induced. Nevertheless, if one happens to consult their conscience while in the shower by silently re-examining h/her own failings and wrongdoings, then there would be no harm in this. However, if one begins to make audible supplications then as long as the place is clean (free from impurities and the bathroom is not immediately adjacent to the toilet) and one's *`awra* (nakedness) is covered, then strictly speaking it would not be unlawful but perhaps better avoided.[323]

And Allah knows best.

43] Using a Ewer

Q. Is using a bodna allowed?

A.

Yes. It is an object used to carry water in order to help in *istinja'*.

And Allah knows best.

---

[323] See Mufti Ludhianvi, *Ahsan al-Fatawa*, 2:36.

44] The Excused Person (*al-ma`dhur*)

Q. How do I know whn [*sic.*] I fall under the rules of being excused. Especially when it comes to bleeding.

A.

If a person suffers any continuous bodily discharge such as blood, gas, urine, faeces, vaginal discharge, etc. that is the duration for one whole *waqt* (time-period) of a Prayer making the person unable to offer the Prayer of that *waqt*, h/she will be classed as "excused" (*ma`dhur*). Not excused from praying but from repeatedly performing *wudu'*. <u>**Example**</u>:

At Zuhr time, Fulan suffers from constant nose bleeding. He realises that he is unable to offer his prayer while remaining in a state of ritual purity due to his bleeding. If this is the case, Fulan will perform *wudu'* and this *wudu'* will last/be valid for the entire Zuhr time-period (i.e. up until `Asr time) even if he continues to bleed. However, he will have to repeat his *wudu'* **<u>if anything other than his nose bleed invalidates it, e.g. he went to the toilet, vomitted a mouthful, passed gas, secreted pus, etc</u>**.[324]

- If within the prayer time-period, one is able to offer h/her prayer without any bleeding or the *wudu'* being invalidated, that person will not be classed as *ma`dhur*, e.g. `Asr begins at 5:00pm and between

---

[324] See al-Tumurtashi's *Tanwir al-Absar* as per al-Haskafi, *Durr al-Mukhtar*, 1:305-306:

ان استوعب عذره تمام وقت صلوة مفروضة بأن لا يجد في جميع وقتها زمنا يتوضأ و يصلي فيه خاليا عن الحدث

و حكمه الوضوء لكل فرض ثم يصلي فيه فرضا و نفلا فاذا خرج الوقت بطل

Zuhr and 5:00pm prayer was possible without *wudu'* being invalidated.

- If one is classed as a *ma`dhur*, one *wudu'* will be sufficient for the entire Prayer time-period unless the *wudu'* was invalidated due to other than the reason of the illness/medical condition.

- If one is classed as a *ma`dhur* for one prayer time-period, he will be automatically classed as a *ma`dhur* for subsequent prayer times **as long as the discharge occurs once in that prayer time**, e.g. Fulan was classed as *ma`dhur* for Zuhr time because of his nose bleed. He will also be *ma`dhur* for `Asr, Maghrib, `Isha', etc. as long as he suffers one instance of his nose bleed in those time periods.

- The *wudu'* of a *ma`dhur* will be valid for the duration of an entire prayer time-period, i.e. until it ends wherein a person can pray any number of prayers, touch the Qur'an, etc.[325]

And Allah knows best.

---

[325] al-Tahtawi, *al-Hashiya*, p.150:

(ولا يصير) من ابتلي بناقض (معذورا حتى يستوعبه العذر وقتا كاملا ليس فيه انقطاع) لعذره (بقدر الوضوء والصلاة) فلو وجد لا يكون معذورا (وهذا) الاستيعاب الحقيقي بوجود العذر في جميع الوقت والاستيعاب الحكمي بالانقطاع القليل الذي لا يسع الطهارة والصلاة (شرط ثبوته) أي العذر (وشرط دوامه) أي العذر (وجوده) أي العذر (في كل وقت بعد ذلك) الاستيعاب الحقيقي أو الحكمي (ولو) كان وجوده (مرة) واحدة ليعلم بها بقاؤه (وشرط انقطاعه وخروج صاحبه عن كونه معذورا خلو وقت كامل عنه) بانقطاعه حقيقة فهذه الثلاث شروط الثبوت والدوام والانقطاع

KEY REFERENCES

English References:

Desai, Ebrahim. *Contemporary Fatawa*, Durban: Darul Iftaa, 2012.

Elias, Afzal Hoosen. *Perform Wudu Correctly*, Lahore: Idara-e-Islamiyat, n.d.

Arabic References:

Ibn 'Abidin, *Hashiyat Radd al-Muhtar 'ala 'l-Durr al-Mukhtar Sharh Tanwir al-Absar*, 7 vols. Beirut: Dar al-Ihya' al-Turath al-'Arabi, n.d.

——— *Radd al-Muhtar 'ala 'l-Durr al-Mukhtar*, 8 vols. Karachi: H. M. S. Co., 1986.

al-'Asqalani, *Fath al-Bari Sharh Sahih al-Bukhari* (Baz and 'Abd al-Baqi edn.), 15 vols. Beirut: Dar al-Kutub al-'Ilmiyya, 1997.

al-Haythami, *Majma' al-Zawa'id*, Cairo: Maktbat al-Qudsi, n.d.

——— al-Haythami, *Majma' al-Zawa'id*, Beirut: Dar al-Kitab al-'Arabi, 1982.

Ibn al-Humam, *Fath al-Qadir li 'l-'Ajiz al-Faqir Sharh al-Hidaya*, 9 vols. Beirut: Dar al-Ihya' al-Turath al-'Arabi, 1997.

al-Kasani, *al-Bada'i' al-Sana'i' fi Tartib al-Shara'i'*, 6 vols. Beirut: Dar al-Ihya' al-Turath al-'Arabi, 2000.

al-Marghinani, *al-Hidaya Sharh Bidyat al-Mubtadi'*, 4 vols. Beirut: Dar al-Kutub al-'Ilmiyya, 2000.

Mawlana Nizam, et al. *al-Fatawa al-Hindiyya*, 6 vols. Quetta: Maktaba Majdiyya, 1983.

———— *al-Fatawa al-Hindiyya*, repr. Beirut: Dar al-Fikr, 1979.

———— *al-Fatawa al-Hindiyya*, 6 vols. Beirut: Dar Ihya' Turath al-'Arabi, 1980.

al-Mawsili, *Kitab al-Ikhtiyar li-Ta'lil al-Mukhtar*, 5 vols. Cairo: Dar al-Ma'rifa, 2000.

al-Maydani, *al-Lubab fi Sharh al-Kitab*, 4 vols. Karachi: Kutub Khana, n.d.

al-Nawawi, *Sharh Sahih Muslim*, 18 vols. Beirut: Dar Ihya' al-Turath al-'Arabi, 1972.

Ibn Nujaym, *al-Bahr al-Ra'iq fi Sharh Kanz al-Daqa'iq*, 9 vols. Beirut: Dar al-Kutub al-'Ilmiyya, 1997.

al-Qal'aji, M. et al, *Mu'jam al-Lughat al-Fuqaha'*, Beirut: Dar al-Nafa'is, 2000.

al-Quduri, *al-Mukhtasar* (English-Arabic text, trans. M. Kiani, London: Dar al-Taqwa, 2009).

al-Shurunbulali, *Nur al-Idah* (English-Arabic text, trans. W. Charkawi) n.p. 2004.

———— *Maraqi al-Falah Sharh Nur al-Idah*, Damascus: Maktabat al-'Ilm al-Hadith, 2001.

———— *Maraqi al-Falah Sharh Nur al-Idah*, Beirut: Dar al-Kutub al-'Ilmiyya, 1995.

———— *Imdad al-Fattah Sharh Nur al-Idah*, Damascus, n.p. 2001.

———— *Maraqi al-Sa'adat*, Beirut: Dar al-Kutub al-Lubnani, 1973 and English trans. by F. A. Khan, London: Whitethread Press, 2010.

———— *Sabil al-Falah fi Sharh Nur al-Idah*, Beirut: Dar al-Bayruti, n.d.

Usmani, M. T. *Takmilat Fath al-Mulhim*, 3 vols. Karachi: Maktabat-i Dar al-'Ulum, 1986-1987.

Urdu References:

Farid, Muhammad. *Fatawa Faridiyya*, 5 vols. Pakistan: Dar al-'Ulum Publications, 2004-2009.

Gangohi, Mahmud Hasan, *Fatawa Mahmudiyya*, 25 vols. Karachi: Dar al-Ifta' Jamia Faruqiyya, n.d.

Jalalpuri, Sa'id Ahmad. *Fatawa Khatme Nabuwwat*, 3 vols. Multan: Alim-e Majlis Khatme Nabuwwat, 2005.

Khan, Ahmed Reza. *al-'Ataya li-Nabawiyya fi' l-Fatawa al-Ridwiyya*, 6 vols. Mubarakpur: Sunni Darul Isha'at, 1981.

———— *al-'Ataya al-Nabawiyya fi' l-Fatawa al-Ridwiyya*, 12 vols. Faisalabad: Maktaba Nuriyya Ridwiyya.

Khan, Muhammad Shu'ayb Allah. *al-Qawl al-Qawi fi Ahkam al-Madhi*, Bangalore, n.d.

Kifayatullah, Muhammad. *Kifayat al-Mufti*, 10 vols. Karachi: Dar al-Isha'at, 2001.

Lajpuri, Abd al-Rahim. *Fatawa Rahimiyya*, 10 vols. Karachi: Darul Isha'at, 2009.

Ludhianvi, Rashid Ahmad. *Ahsan al-Fatawa*, Karachi: H. M. S. Co, 1398–.

Ludhianvi, Muhammad Yusuf. *Apke Masa'il Aur Unka Hal*, 10 vols. Karachi: Maktabat al-Ludhianwi, 1995-2002.

Qasmi, Mujahid al-Islam. *Fatawa Qadi*, Delhi: IFA Publications, 2004.

Qasimi, Muhammad Rif'at. *Masa'il-e Khuffayn*, Lahore: Maktabat-e Khalil, 1415 A.H.

——— *Masa'il-e Rif'at Qasimi*, 7 vols. Karachi: Khadim-e Kutub Khana. 1429 A.H.

Sahranpuri, Khalil Ahmad. *Fatawa Mazahir 'Ulum* (= *Fatawa Khaliliyya*), Karachi: Maktabat Shaykh, n.d.

Sakarvi, 'Abd al-Ra'uf. *Masa'il-e Ghusl*, Karachi: Maktabat Dar al-'Ulum, 1398 A.H.

Shams al-Haqq, *Ahkam-e Taharat*, Sultanabad: Madrasat al-Hikma Trust, 2006.

Usmani, Zafar Ahmad. *Imdad al-Ahkam*, 4 vols. Sahranpur: Deoband Publications, 1991.

Usmani, Kafil al-Rahman. *Siraj al-Idah Sharh Nur al-Idah*, Multan: Kutub Khana Majidiyya, n.d.

NOTES

www.ingramcontent.com/pod-product-compliance
Lightning Source LLC
Chambersburg PA
CBHW051504170526
45166CB00001B/384